Performance Appraisal

Source Book

Performance Appraisal
Source Book

A Collection of Practical Samples

Mike Deblieux

Society for Human Resource Management
Alexandria, Virginia
USA
www.shrm.org

The Society for Human Resource Management (SHRM) is the world's largest association devoted to human resource management. Representing more than 225,000 members in over 130 countries, the Society serves the needs of HR professionals and advances the interests of the HR profession. Founded in 1948, SHRM has more than 575 affiliated chapters within the United States and subsidiary offices in China and India. Visit SHRM Online at **www.shrm.org**.

Library of Congress Cataloging-in-Publication Data

Deblieux, Michael.
 Performance appraisal source book : a collection of practical samples
/ Mike Deblieux.
     p. cm.
 Includes index.
 ISBN 1-58644-037-3
 1. Employees--Rating of. I. Title.
HF5549.5.R3 D37 2003
658.3'125--dc21

                                2002153046

Printed in the United States of America.
10 9 8 7 6   12-0607

Dedication

This book is dedicated to my father, Henry Roy Deblieux, Jr. (1925–2002). The principles of hard work, dedication, and curiosity that he taught me during his life are deeply ingrained in who I am and what I am. Let us always remember that his service and the service of his generation in World War II protected the freedom that allows us to freely exchange ideas like the ones in this book.

Contents

Figures/Sample Forms

Figures

Sample Forms

Preface

I received my first performance review while working as an administrative intern during my last year of college. The human resources (HR) manager called me into his office. He dropped a piece of paper on his desk and said, "Here, you need to sign this so I can put it in your file." I can still see the words scrawled in his doctor-like handwriting on that piece of paper: "Mike is an outstanding intern." I signed the form and handed it back to him. He handed me a copy and said, "Congratulations!" That was it. That was my first review.

My need for more information got the best of me that day. I returned to my desk and wrote a memo to the HR manager. I asked him for more specific feedback. I was beckoned back to his office in a nanosecond. I received a short, but firm lecture about not questioning the word of an experienced manager.

I learned four important lessons that morning. First, the things I was reading and learning in college were not all true in the real world that I was about to enter. Second, I learned that I really wanted to know how the boss thought I was doing. I didn't want generalities: I wanted specifics. My boss's evaluation was important to me, particularly at that stage of my career. Third, I learned that managers do not like it when you question their judgment. Fourth, I learned that there had to be a better way. I didn't know what it was at the time, but I knew it had to be out there somewhere.

Don't get me wrong—that HR manager was one of the best supervisors in my career. He was a mentor and, now retired, remains a friend. That experience opened a door for me. It started me on an expedition to read, question, and explore the topic of performance management. It resulted in six books before this one, various articles, and countless workshops on the topic.

I love helping HR professionals, managers, and employees look at the process of performance reviews. It is a great challenge to get them to question their own paradigms about what a performance review is and to imagine what it could be. When Laura Lawson, Manager of Book Publishing at SHRM, invited me to update and add to this book, I jumped at the chance. Her call gave me an opportunity to share my ideas with you in hopes that you will find that better way that I sought at the beginning of my career. I thank her for the opportunity and for the support that she has provided throughout this project.

A special thank-you goes to the HR specialists who staff SHRM's HR Knowledge Center. The Knowledge Center pioneered the book on which this one is based, and the Center staff helped immeasurably in collecting the sample forms for this book.

Sincere thanks go to the legal reviewers of the manuscript and forms: Jonathan A. Segal, Wolf, Block, Schorr, & Solis-Cohen; and Teresa Tracy of Baker & Hostetler. Also thanks go to Sharon K. Koss, SPHR, CCP, Koss Management Consulting, for reviewing the manuscript from a human-resources perspective.

Finally, I thank all of the organizations that contributed forms for consideration, and especially the following organizations and their HR professionals, whose forms are the heart of this book: Alpine Electronics of America, Inc.; Amazon.com, Inc.; Apriso Corporation; Atlas Material Testing Technology, LLC; Attachmate; Ball Horticultural Company; BlueCross BlueShield of North Carolina; Cargill Dow LLC; Citistreet, TBO; Colorado Asthma & Allergy Centers P.C.; Corvette America; FAST, Inc.; Ford & Harrison LLP; FPIC Insurance Group, Inc.; Gateway HomeCare, Inc.; GSE Systems, Inc.; Health Partners; The Human Resource Professional Group/HRPG; Johnsonville Sausage; Level Valley Creamery, Inc.; MemberWorks, Inc.; Merricks, Inc.; MusicMatch; NetManage; The Newberry Group, Inc.; Oak-Leyden Development Services, Inc.; Portala Packaging, Inc.; Prince Industries, Inc.; Rea & Associates, Inc.; Sammamish Plateau Water & Sewer District; Slakey Brothers; Tokyo Electron, Inc.; The Urology Group; and Zellweger Analytics, Inc.

Introduction

A performance review is one piece of a performance management system. An effective performance management system includes a number of components:

- Employee input and participation in developing performance expectations.

- Communicating performance expectations before the performance review period starts.

- Ongoing positive and constructive feedback and communication about progress toward established goals throughout the review period.

- Consideration and use of specific work samples from throughout the performance review period to provide feedback.

- Input from co-workers, customers, and others who work with the employee on a day-to-day basis.

- Feedback that shows the employee how to perform successfully in the future.

The question is, Why does the performance review form get so much attention? The answer is that it is the most visible part of the performance management process. You can see it, touch it, and talk about it. You can have an opinion about it. You can have a better one from a previous employer. It is not as easy to compare the planning, coaching, and record keeping that lead up to the point of writing a review. Managers deal with tremendous pressures and variables every day, one employee at a time. But sooner or later, the myriad of their unique experiences comes down to the common task of filling out a performance review form. That shared experience makes the form easy prey for criticism. While the form is the focus of this book, five introductory chapters have been added to this edition to help you look at the process and the system that goes with it.

Without a doubt, the most important thing I can say to you as you begin this book is to remember that there is no perfect form. The ideal form has not been and never will be developed. It cannot be. Your organization, your workforce, and your workplace environment are different from the organization, workforce, and workplace environment across the street. The question is not whether any of the forms in this book will work for you and your organization. The question is, How can you best *adapt* pieces of the forms in this book, based on your understanding of your organization, to produce a form that works best for your managers and employees?

The second most important thing to be thinking about is that it is critical for you to include the input and ideas of employees in your planning process. The employee is the "customer" in the performance management system. If the system does not make sense to the customer, it won't work. They won't like it. They will not buy into it and they will not support it. Except for the newest of new employees in his or her very first job, all employees have opinions about performance reviews. If you ask them, they will tell you. Ask them. Listen to them. Learn from them, and then begin to build your system.

An effective performance management system is based on an organizational commitment to communicate openly and honestly about the expectations of managers and the contributions of employees. It includes employees as partners in the process. It provides managers with an effective tool to establish performance goals and objectively monitor employees' performances toward them. It is based on a day-to-day practice of providing feedback that rewards performance contributions and seeks to correct performance problems. It uses performance information from the past to predict, guide, and correct performance in the future. Most important, it is never finished. Like a thermostat, an effective performance management system always involves checking performance contributions to help employees make minor adjustments that improve job performance. Whether you are designing, refining, or redesigning a performance management system, you need to consider each of these elements carefully.

This book is designed to help you plan your performance management system and the performance review form or forms that will bring it to life. Part 1 includes five chapters. Chapter One introduces you to the concept of performance reviews. It gives you some background and logic to help you draw a blueprint of the system you will ultimately recommend. Chapter Two explains some of the legal issues you need to consider as you develop and implement your system. Chapter Three gives you some tips on how to implement your new or revised system. It shows you how to work with managers to help them accept and use your system effectively. Chapter Four focuses on some of the key pitfalls that cause problems for managers, employees, and human resources professionals. Chapter Five completes the cycle by helping you to give managers the tools they need to set goals for future performance.

Part 2 provides a smorgasbord of performance review forms, compiled through the generous contributions of HR professionals. The forms represent the best of what these professionals have developed and are using in their organizations.

Part 1:
Performance Reviews

Chapter One:
Designing a Performance Review System

Before you design a performance review system, it is important to know why you want one in the first place. Historically, human resources (HR) professionals have designed and implemented performance reviews for a variety of reasons, including the following:

- Justifying employees' pay increases.

- Documenting concerns about employee job performance.

- Protecting the organization from legal challenges to discipline and termination actions.

- Formally showing employees that the organization cares about them.

- Providing a record of performance for managers to consider when they are thinking about promoting or transferring an employee.

- Providing a consistent tool for coaching employees.

All these reasons have some merit. They also have some problems. For example, some would argue that requiring a performance review to be written is the best way to ensure that pay increases are indeed based on job performance. Others would argue that the review and the raise are separate and distinct issues and discussions. Both groups could be right. Some would argue that a performance review could save an employer millions of dollars in a wrongful termination suit by documenting examples of performance deficiencies. Others would argue that a review could cost the employer millions by inadvertently painting a picture of satisfactory or better performance for an ineffective employee. Again, both groups could be right. The chicken or the egg discussion could go on forever. Each organization needs to evaluate these issues and decide which answers are best for it.

■ Reasons for Doing a Performance Review

While many of the reasons for doing a performance review are debatable, there are three reasons that managers and HR professionals should be able to agree upon:

- Clarifying job duties, performance expectations, and goals.

- Summarizing past performance discussions.

- Providing a blueprint for future performance.

Let us look at each of these reasons to help you start thinking about what you want to accomplish with the performance review system you are designing or revising.

Clarifying Job Duties, Performance Expectations, and Goals

A performance review is about a job and how well it is being performed. It is a good place to talk about what the job is. The performance review provides an opportunity for the manager and the employee to focus on what the manager expects and how the employee can provide it. It is a time when telephone calls, e-mails, and other interruptions are a second priority. It is a time to talk about why the position exists and whether the money being spent on it is producing the result management had in mind.

The manager and the employee should each have a clear and consistent understanding of the employee's job duties long before the performance review is written and presented. From the beginning of the review period, the employee should know how the manager expects the job to be performed. The performance review should not be the first place that these issues are discussed. It is a place, however, where the manager and employee can openly discuss and work to better understand what is expected and how it is being done.

Another reason for talking about these issues is that performance expectations are not set in concrete. Jobs change during the year for two reasons. First, the manager makes new assignments or takes away old ones. Second, the employee voluntarily takes on new work or stops doing current work. The performance review provides an opportunity to review those changes to make sure that they were intended and they are expected to continue.

You might say that the manager and the employee should be talking about these things on an ongoing basis throughout the year. Indeed they should. But if you watch closely, those discussions, when they do take place, are most often about a specific project, deadline, or problem. They are often sandwiched in between other issues and conducted on the run. The performance review provides an opportunity to put those discussions in context. It provides an opportunity to summarize them in relationship to the job itself.

In some organizations, the manager and the employee are required to go over the job description and reach agreement on what it should say at the beginning of the review period and again before the review is written. This meeting of the minds helps to focus the employee on the proper job priorities. Even if an organization does not have a written job description for every position, there is one in the mind of the manager and the employee. Think about it this way. If we meet at a party and I ask you what you do in your job, you will give me a list of your major job duties. If I have lunch with your manager and ask what your role is in the organization, your manager will give me a list of your job duties. Each of you tells me what you think the job is, but have you told each other? The performance review provides an opportunity for the manager and the employee to have that discussion in a structured and purposeful environment.

Summarizing Past Performance Discussions

Managers like to think that they keep their employees well informed about the quality of their work. In fact, however, they often do not. Many employees report that their manager could improve at giving performance feedback.

In my extension classes at the University of California, Irvine, I often ask HR students to interview employees at work and ask them about their relationship with their managers. I ask them to come up with a list of their own questions, but I require two questions to be on every list. The first question is, How do you know when you are doing a good job? In nearly twenty years of reading the papers that result from this assignment, I have concluded that the average employee answers with, "No one has told me otherwise, so I assume I am doing the right thing." Some are more direct. They answer with, "No one has yelled at me lately!" While positive feedback should occur regularly, the performance review provides a unique opportunity to provide specific feedback about what is being done right, why it is right, and why it is important to continuing doing it in the future.

The second question I ask students is, How do you know when you are not doing your job correctly? The typical answer is, "I usually do not until long after it is possible to do anything about it." Another oft-repeated answer is, "I find out about it when all of corporate head-quarters is at my desk to tell me about it!" That should not happen, but it does. The courts are full of cases to prove it. The discussion of a performance problem should occur at the time the mistake is made. A performance review provides an opportunity to put the mistake in the context of overall performance. If progress has been made to correct the problem, the manager should acknowledge it, express appreciation for it, and encourage the employee to continue it. If progress has not been made, the manager must confront the issue, work with the employee to redefine the expectations, and continue to follow up until the issue is resolved.

One of the dangers of summarizing past performance is that the discussion can be too general. Your system must be designed to help the manager and the employee discuss specific examples of performance. Unfortunately, the discussion is often based on common but vague expressions, such as the following:

> You do a great job with customers.
>
> I can always depend on you.
>
> You need to get on the ball.
>
> Some people think you have a bad attitude.

The employee can do little with this information. The first two examples are positive comments that will most likely result in a nervous "Thank you" from the employee. The second two are intended to be constructive. Unfortunately, they are so general that the employee will most likely be either bewildered or angered by them.

If your system is going to work, it must include a mechanism for tracking examples of performance during the review period. Managers need to be encouraged to keep notes, work samples, and other performance information to help them remember key events.

Providing a Blueprint for Future Performance

If there is any one reason for having a performance review system, it is to provide direction for future performance. If it is important to discuss performance expectations when an employee is new, it is even more important to discuss them periodically throughout the employee's career. The performance review provides a mechanism for that discussion.

Your system should be designed to ensure that improved future performance is its primary goal. In fact, your system's success should be measured by the quality of future performance. Past performance cannot be changed. If an employee leaves the discussion focused only on past performance, the review, the review system, and the manager have failed. Managers must make a planned and concerted effort to help the employee use the review of past performance to succeed in the future.

Your system must include an element that communicates future expectations. It can be in the body of the review or it can be at the end of it, but it must be there. The manager can expect the employee to maintain current performance levels, improve or correct performance deficiencies, or accept changing or different assignments for the future.

In many cases, the employee is doing exactly what he or she is supposed to be doing. There is no need to change it. The manager's challenge is to communicate satisfaction with that performance and to encourage the employee to keep performing at that level. In other cases, change is an important future goal. If the review of past performance shows that the efforts to correct performance deficiencies have not been successful, the future expectation must clearly be to correct those deficiencies. In still other cases, the employee's future will involve new or different performance tasks (for example, working on a new computer system) or levels (for example, higher sales goals). Those expected changes are part of looking into the future. They must be communicated clearly.

■ Getting Started

There are several steps you should follow to develop your new system and the forms that go along with it:

- ▓   Understand the organization and the workforce.

- ▓   Understand the current system.

- ▓   Gather information on employee preferences.

- ▓   Gather information on manager preferences and practices.

- ▓   Design the review and related tools.

- ▓   Implement it.

Understand the Organization and the Workforce

Start by taking a close look at your organization and your workforce. A software firm is different from an accounting firm. A hospital is different from a manufacturing plant. While the common goal is to give feedback on performance, the culture, the diversity, and the occupational makeup of the workforce will have a lot to do with the design and success of your system. A sample questionnaire to get you started is shown in **Figure 1**. Use it to develop a plan for looking carefully at your organization.

Figure 1   Checklist: The Organization and the Workforce

1. **The workforce** (Enter percentage of total workforce; should add up to 100%.)

   Education

   ___ %   ___ %   ___ %   ___ %   ___ %
   HS not completed   Completed HS   Some college   BA or BS   MA, MS, or above

   Tenure (in this organization)

   ___ %   ___ %   ___ %   ___ %   ___ %
   Less than one year   More than one but   More than three but   More than five but   More than ten years
                   less than three years   less than five years   less than ten years

2. **The work** (Enter percentage of total workforce; should add up to 100%.)

   ___ %   ___ %   ___ %   ___ %   ___ %
   Officials and managers   Professionals   Technicians   Sales workers   Office and clerical workers

   ___ %   ___ %   ___ %   ___ %
   Craft workers (skilled)   Operatives (semi-skilled)   Laborers (unskilled)   Service workers

3. **Communication practices** (Rank in order of most frequent use; "1" is most frequent.)

   What is the primary method of communicating workplace issues?
   ___ Written (paper)   ___ Written (electronic)   ___ Telephone   ___ In person   ___ Other
   _____

   What is the predominate style for addressing workplace issues?
   ___ We don't   ___ Supervisors and   ___ Boss is always right   ___ Just depends   ___ Other
               employees work together   _____

4. **Management philosophy** (Rank in order of most frequent use; "1" is most frequent.)

   How does management operate on workplace issues?
   ___ One-size fits all   ___ Consistent practice   ___ Policy determined   ___ Some subjects or   ___ Other
                       where appropriate   by individual managers   issues are untouchable   _____

   How does management respond to HR initiative?
   ___ Accepted with   ___ Tolerated with   ___ Depends on   ___ General opposition   ___ Other
   great enthusiasm   sporadic support   the issue

5. **Other issues**

   List any other style or practice issues that affect communication about workplace issues.

   _____

   _____

   _____

One of the key issues you will want to consider is how the organization's staff members normally communicate. Communication practices tell you a lot about how to set up your performance management system. For example, a fast food restaurant's employees do not normally communicate with memoranda or even e-mails. Much of the communication is verbal. A multistep process and lengthy form would probably not work effectively. On the other hand, a bank depends on written communication to fulfill its mission. Managers and employees read and in many cases write detailed and even complex messages. The successful review system for the bank would be very different from the one for the fast food restaurant.

It is important to consider the makeup of the workforce. The staff's education, experience, and occupations will have a lot to do with how you design your system. If your organization includes a wide array of education, experience, and occupational levels, you may find that it is best to have different systems in different parts of the organization. For example, a 360-degree review process may work exceptionally well for the teams in your manufacturing plant, but it may be a disaster in the accounting department.

It is also important to understand the management style and practices of the leaders in your workplace. In one organization, you may find that nobody does anything until everyone agrees that it is the right thing to do. In another organization, you may find that each manager runs an independent fiefdom where little or no concern is given to the needs, wants, and desires of the rest of the organization.

For example, in one organization, one manager boldly stated that no one would ever get the highest possible performance rating in his department. Another manager stated just as boldly that her goal was to make sure that every employee in her department was rated at the top of the scale and that she considered any manager who had any less of a goal as incompetent! The chief executive officer (CEO) was totally unwilling to step between them. If you are the HR professional designing that organization's review system, you need to consider those differences as you design the system.

Understand the Current System

The easiest and probably the most informative place to start analyzing the current system is to collect all of the forms related to performance reviews. In some cases, the forms will be in an electronic format. You should print them out for easy reference and analysis. It is important to include the personnel action notice and other forms or computer screens that may be used to document performance feedback or the result of performance feedback. Look for forms or processes where employees are asked for their input before or after the review is prepared. Collect documents or screens that may be used to ask employees to provide feedback to their managers on their management style.

You should gather a copy of each performance review form that is used in the organization. Be sure to look around and see if individual managers or departments have adopted their own ad hoc forms or practices. It is important for you to ask lots of questions to help you understand them and why they are used.

Next, spend some time in the filing system, whether paper or electronic. You should carefully examine a cross section of reviews and other forms that have been completed under the current system. Look to see if they result in objective, job-related feedback. Ask yourself if the system creates repetitious or confusing feedback. Most important, ask if the feedback helps the employee to move forward or if it focuses too heavily on past issues that cannot be changed.

It is important to develop a clear picture of how the current system came into being. In one company, a production manager had designed a review form ten years earlier. No one liked it, but everyone was afraid to challenge it because the manager was seen as a strong, opinionated leader. In another company, the founder and CEO had developed a thirteen-page document that covered every possible performance and career factor in the life of an employee. The form was beautiful but not useful. While everyone saw problems with the form, no one wanted to confront the CEO. It is important to know where these skeletons are before you start redesigning a system. **Figure 2** will give you some ideas about what to look for in the current system.

Gather Information on Employee Preferences

Finding out about employee preferences may be the most important part of your project. Employees are the customers in a performance review system. You really need to know what they want and the form they want it in. If they will not buy it, there is not much point in manufacturing it.

Develop a plan to interview individual employees to learn about their expectations for a performance review. Be careful to solicit individual input rather than representative input. You are not asking an individual to tell you how others feel. You are asking a cross sample of individuals to tell you about their experiences with performance management in this and other organizations. As you talk to variety of people, you will begin to see a pattern of expectations within your organization.

It is a good idea to start the discussion by asking what aspects of the performance review system employees think work well. People always have lots to say about what does not work. You can save that for later in the conversation. Try to help interviewees focus on what they want as opposed to what they do not want in a performance management system. Help them to look at each aspect of their experience. Ask them to describe what they remember and liked about starting as new employees. Ask them how they learned about what would be expected of them in their new job. Walk them through their first review cycle and subsequent annual reviews.

In this discussion, if employees begin to talk about their frustrations or disappointments, try to get them to come back to what they liked about the process. Let them know that they will have an opportunity later to tell you what they did not like.

Figure 2   Checklist: The Current System

1. **The Policy** (Check all that apply.)

Is a policy currently in effect?   ❏ yes   ❏ no

Does the current policy provide for:
❏ Providing a copy of the review form to new employees   ❏ A review in the first 30, 60, or 90 days of employment
❏ A midyear review   ❏ An annual review on the employee's anniversary
❏ An annual review at the same time for all employees

Are pay increases:
❏ Linked to performance reviews   ❏ Done separately from performance reviews

How does the policy provide for employee input?
❏ It doesn't   ❏ With a form   ❏ Left to individual managers   ❏ Not permitted

What is the approval process for performance reviews?
❏ Manager only   ❏ Manager and HR   ❏ Manager, director or VP, and HR   ❏ Management committee

2. **Forms** (Check all that apply.)

What forms are used in the current system?

New employee	❏ Paper	❏ Computer
Introductory period review	❏ Paper	❏ Computer
Midyear review	❏ Paper	❏ Computer
Annual review	❏ Paper	❏ Computer
Personnel action notice	❏ Paper	❏ Computer
Employee input	❏ Paper	❏ Computer
Performance planner for supervisors	❏ Paper	❏ Computer
Disciplinary action notice	❏ Paper	❏ Computer

3. **Practice** (Fill in the percentages and numbers.)

Given a random sample of 50 reviews, what percentage are on time?
____ % on time   ____ % late

How many managers who report to the top level of management received reviews at their last review date?
____ # of direct reports to top management   ____ # who received reviews at last due date

Describe how performance reviews are approved under the current system.

_____

_____

_____

_____

Again, it is important to keep in mind that you are conducting research at this stage. Ask lots of questions to be sure you understand what you are hearing. Here are some questions you might ask:

> Can you give me a specific example of a time when it worked that way?

> What did you like about the way your manager gave you constructive feedback?

> Would you recommend that we try to adopt a process like that in this organization?

> Were managers trained to do it that way, or was this something that just your manager did?

> Have you worked for other organizations or managers that did it this way? Was it just as successful in those organizations?

Once you have a clear picture of what each individual liked about his previous experiences, you can explore what he did not like. Be careful here. It is very important to separate the system or the process from the personal experience of the individual. For example, an employee who received a negative review may tell you that the entire system is flawed. Her statement may be based on a very natural defensive mechanism. It is important to probe deeper to find out how the system actually worked. Let us look at such an interview to give you some ideas:

> **Interviewer:** That gives me some really good ideas about what you liked about the review system there. Were there any things that you did not like about the system?

> **Employee:** Oh yeah. There was plenty of that.

> **Interviewer:** What would be one example?

> **Employee:** I had one supervisor who was a real loser when it came to reviews. I got the worst ratings I ever had in my whole life from her. She was totally unrealistic in what she expected.

> **Interviewer:** Can you be more specific?

> **Employee:** Sure. We got a new computer system. It was a mess from the beginning. All of us struggled with it. Even the managers had a hard time with it. Instead of giving me credit for trying to work through the bugs, she wrote on my review that I was resistant to change. That wasn't true at all.

> **Interviewer:** Why do you think she put that on the form?

> **Employee:** Well, there was a section labeled something like "areas for future improvement." She told me that she had to put something there to make HR happy so that was what she decided to write. I started looking for a new job the next day.

In this example, the interviewer learned a number of things:

- Sometimes supervisors feel obligated to complete every section of the form, even if a section does not apply.

- Employees expect honest and objective feedback.

- Supervisors need to be trained to use performance management tools correctly.

Figure 3	Sample Employee Interview Questions

How did the review system in your last job work?

_____

_____

How often were you reviewed?   ❏ every ___ months   ❏ every ___ years

What did you like about the system at your last employer?

_____

_____

What did you dislike about the system at your last employer?

_____

_____

How long have you worked here?   _____ months   _____ years

Have you been given a review here?   ❏ yes   ❏ no

What did you like about your review?

_____

_____

What did you dislike about your review?

_____

_____

Is there anything you would suggest we do differently with reviews?

_____

_____

There is no magic number of employees to interview. It all depends on the size and diversity of your organization. It is important to talk to enough people to begin to get a feel for the issues that concern them and the type of feedback that they prefer to receive from their managers. **Figure 3** gives you some ideas of questions to ask.

Gather Information on Manager Preferences and Practices

Interviewing managers is very similar to interviewing employees. You want to find out what they like and do not like about the current system. You want to hear what they think about other systems they have used in other organizations. You also want to find

Figure 4	Sample Manager Interview Questions

What has been your experience with performance reviews here and in other organizations?

_____

_____

_____

What would you change about our current system?

_____

_____

_____

Have you had any experience with employees giving input to their performance review before it is written? If yes, how has it worked?

_____

_____

_____

Have you had any experience with employees providing feedback to their manager on the manager's performance as a workplace leader? If yes, what was your experience?

_____

_____

_____

Have you had any experience with peers giving feedback on the job performances of their co-workers? If yes, what was your experience?

_____

_____

_____

out if they use or have used any of their own tools or special techniques. In some cases, managers may be able to share samples of those tools from their own files or by calling previous employers to get them for you.

In addition to likes and dislikes about the system, you want to hear managers talk about how much time they have to spend on reviews and whether they think it is a good investment. You want to hear what they think can be done to make feedback more effective and less time-consuming. **Figure 4** gives you some ideas for planning your management interviews.

Design the Performance Review System and Related Tools

At last you are ready to begin designing your system. This book focuses primarily on the performance review tool. For your system to work, however, it is important that you devise a plan and tools that include the entire employment process, including the following aspects:

New employees—Great performance does not start at the end of the introductory period. It does not start with the first review. It starts on the very first day of employment. You should plan to introduce new employees to their job and their manager's expectations. Here are some ideas to help you orient the new employee to the position:

- Welcome packet mailed in advance of the first day—Mail a packet of information to the new employee shortly after the job offer is accepted. Include a job description and a copy of the performance review form that will be used to give feedback.

- Performance objectives memo—Prepare a brief memo for each new employee that outlines the key factors that will be used to evaluate performance during the first ninety days of employment.

- Performance objectives meeting—Establish a practice of managers meeting with new employees to discuss the performance objectives memo or other performance expectations on the first or second day on the job.

Promotions and transfers—Your system should be designed to support promoted and transferred employees in much the same way that it supports new employees. When people move to a new job, they need to find out what is expected of them sooner rather than later. You cannot just hope that it will happen; you need to plan for it. The ideas listed above for the new employee can be easily adapted for the promoted or transferred employee.

System or process changes—Organizations today are always looking for new and better ways to work. Part of planning for those changes includes preparing employees to accept them and perform within them. Your system must include a method for defining the new work and the expectations that go with it.

Performance deficiencies—It is one thing to say that a performance review should not contain any surprises. It is another to provide managers with the tools they need to address performance problems. Your system must include tools that help managers coach employees through performance issues. It must help them to take appropriate corrective action, up to and including termination, when appropriate.

You will have to make some important decisions about how you want the reviews to work. Here are the key decisions you will have to make:

Format of performance reviews—The forms in Part 2 of this book will give you several formats to consider. You will see two basic formats. One is based on job traits (for example, job knowledge, quantity of work, quality of work). This format has the advantage of working for all jobs, from CEO to sales representative. It has the disadvantage of requiring the manager to fit comments into a category that may not be a perfect fit. For example, "quantity of work" might work well for an assembly worker but be almost impossible to apply to a research technician. In addition, it tends to result in generic comments from managers.

The other format is based on job duties. It has the advantage of being job specific. It asks the manager to provide feedback on each of the major job duties assigned to the employee. It has the disadvantage of requiring a separate form for each job classification.

Frequency of reviews—HR professionals often debate how often an employee should receive a performance review. Should it be once a year, twice a year, or more often? The answer is whatever is right for your organization. If you are in a fairly static environment where the work of most employees does not change significantly throughout the year, an annual review is probably sufficient. If employees perform project work (for example, at an accounting firm), it may be best to give employees a review at the end of each major project. In a high-volume environment, it may be appropriate to provide quarterly reviews. In most organizations where a review is given more than once a year, the main review is more thorough than the off-cycle reviews.

The desires and needs of employees should also be taken into consideration. In some organizations, the policy requires that employees be given an annual review but permits them to request additional off-cycle reviews during the year.

Ratings in reviews—A rating system, in whatever form it takes, summarizes the manager's evaluation of the employee's performance in a few well-chosen words. It places the manager's perspective on a scale from high to low. It can be used to compare employee performance among employees, departments, or even geographic locations.

The main purpose of a performance review is to help the employee perform successfully in the future. If your goal is to influence future performance, you need to select ratings that will support your goal. You will see several different rating systems on the forms in Part 2. Consider each of them in relationship to your overall goals for your review system.

Approvals required—Another important issue to consider is how and when a performance review will be approved. In many organizations, an HR professional approves the review before it is given to the employee. The HR professional is trained to watch for comments that might be innocent on the surface but discriminatory in practice. For example, a manager might write, "Mary was a very good employee last year except for the three months she was off to have her daughter." The manager may be innocently trying to indicate that Mary was not at work for the entire year. The HR professional would read the same comment as possible evidence of gender bias or discrimination based on the employee's right to take Family and Medical Leave. The two need to talk about it and take out the comment. If they discover that the manager is trying to make an important point, they need to find another way to make it.

Interestingly, managers sometimes object to HR approving reviews before they are presented to the employee. They see it as infringing on their right to make important decisions about their staff. They are missing the point. There was a time when managers were expected to have all the answers about all the issues involving their employees. In today's world, an effective manager depends on experts in HR to provide an objective perspective on important employee matters.

Employees sometimes object to having HR and/or a higher-level manager approve a review before it is presented to the employee. The employees perceive a review with several signatures already on it as being final and irrevocable. They believe that it is fruitless to raise any concerns about any aspect of the review that they may see as incomplete or inaccurate. An effective system includes a clear appeal or review process to allay such concerns.

Another approval issue is the manager's manager. In most organizations a manager above the employee's immediate manager must approve the review before it is presented. This step is designed to help ensure that the review is technically accurate and fair in relation to feedback that is given to others in the department. It also raises an interesting problem. Sometimes, the senior manager disagrees with the rating or comments of the employee's manager. Your system must include a mechanism for resolving these differences before the review is presented to the employee.

Appeals to reviews—There was a time when employees sat and listened quietly while their manager explained their review. When it was over they stood up and humbly thanked the manager for the valuable feedback. If they disagreed with the review, they kept quiet for fear that it would cost them their jobs. Today, employees increasingly are willing to speak up when they feel a review is inaccurate, unfair, or incomplete. An appeal process gives employees a way to have an objective party listen to their concerns without having to go outside the organization.

The first appeal should be back to the employee's immediate manager. (However, employees must be permitted to bypass their managers if they believe the manager has engaged in unlawful discrimination, harassment, or retaliation.)

The purpose of the review should be to (1) listen to the employee's objections and (2) clarify the facts related to the employee's concern. If the employee raises factual issues that were not taken into consideration when the review was prepared, those issues should be considered. If they are accurate, the manager should be willing to change the review. If the employee's information does not change the manager's conclusions, the manager should attempt to help the employee understand the reasons for the statements in the review. You may want the performance review system to provide for one more level of appeal for employees who continue to object.

Upward reviews—Managers spend a lot of time evaluating their subordinates' performances. In some organizations, the reverse is also increasingly common. Employees are given an opportunity to provide their managers with feedback on their performances as workplace leaders. If you decide to include this step in your system, you need to think it through carefully. You need to teach employees how to give objective, job-related feedback on their manager's performance. Likewise, you need to teach managers to receive the feedback objectively and learn to use it to improve their own performances.

Chapter Two:
Legal Considerations

A performance review documents a manager's conclusions about an employee's contributions. Once a performance review is written, signed, and filed, it cannot be taken back. If any of its content is not job related or is inaccurate or unfair, the organization, and possibly the manager, may pay a price in court. Your system must be designed to prevent legal problems. It must include training (see Chapter Three), an audit function to catch inadvertent errors, and an appeal process to allow employees with concerns to express them and get them resolved internally without the need for outside intervention.

■ Keeping Legal Issues in Perspective

Over the years, HR professionals have become increasingly aware of the potential liability associated with managing performance. In some cases that awareness freezes important HR initiatives and prevents progress. You cannot ignore the potential liability, but you also cannot let it prevent you from accomplishing legitimate business goals.

It is important for you to review your plans for your system with a labor attorney who understands your business and the goals you are trying to accomplish. You need to present your entire plan to your counsel and explain how you expect it to work. Ask your counsel if there are any potential problems with your plan. Consider the attorney's feedback and then make final decisions about the system.

■ Putting Manager Performance First

One of the most important legal issues related to performance management is that what the manager has or has not done is often more important than what the employee has or has not done. One important part of a manager's job is to help people within the organization succeed. Helping people succeed involves defining the job, establishing performance standards, training, coaching, giving feedback, and much more. If non-performing employees are able to show that their managers did not do one or more of those things, they can easily claim that their failure to perform is not their fault. Instead, they can blame their managers for not providing them with the tools they need to succeed.

As a result, it is important to give careful thought to how to deal with managers who do not do the performance management portion of their jobs properly. Managers must understand that performance management is not an option but a requirement. They must understand that they are required to use the policies, procedures, forms, and other tools the organization provides to manage employee performance.

■ Maintaining Timeliness

Your policy establishes due dates for performance reviews and other performance management steps. Those due dates are often seen as a commitment or promise that the employer has made to the employee. If the promise is not kept and the failure has an adverse affect on the employee, it may become an issue in a legal proceeding. This is particularly the case when most reviews are completed on time but the review for a difficult or poor-performing employee is late.

Late reviews allow non-performing employees to claim that they were not told about performance problems. They can argue that had they been told about the problems, they would have had an opportunity to correct them. Even if the employees have been told about the problems in other ways (for instance, disciplinary action), they may claim that the late reviews deprived them of feedback that the organization promised in its policies. They can argue that the late or missing performance review contributed to their performance deficiencies.

In addition to potential legal problems, a late review can add to or create morale problems. Employees look to their managers to do what they said they were going to do. If the policy says that an employee will get a review at a certain time, the employee expects the manager to meet the deadline. If the manager does not complete and present the review, the employee begins to question the organization's commitment to its employees.

Here are some steps to take to minimize the risks associated with late reviews and encourage timely ones.

Policy Wording

The policy should say that reviews are due on or about the employee's anniversary date (or whatever due date you establish). This wording allows some leeway for legitimate business delays. It does not allow a review to be several weeks or months late.

Alerts and Reminders

The performance review system should alert managers to the due dates for reviews. Some electronic systems can be set up to send automatic e-mail reminders. One HR professional starts each new calendar year by giving managers small labels with the employee's name and the due date for the review. The labels are accompanied by instructions to place them in the manager's day planner at least six weeks before the review is due.

Corrective Action

When a manager fails to meet an obligation, it is often overlooked. A manager who does not meet performance review deadlines should be coached on the importance of getting reviews done on time. If the problem continues, the manager should be subject to corrective action.

Rewards and Thank-you Notes

Managers who meet deadlines established in the policy should be rewarded. The reward may be as simple as a thank-you note or may involve more formal recognition from a senior manager. At the very least, meeting deadlines should be mentioned as an example of positive performance in the manager's own performance review.

■ Defining Performance Issues

One of the big issues in wrongful termination cases is whether the employee knew or should have known that he or she was not performing properly. Managers tend to define performance issues in general terms, writing and saying statements like this:

> Her customer service skills need some work.
>
> He doesn't seem to understand the basic principles of writing code.
>
> He isn't up to speed yet.
>
> She isn't a team player.

Such statements leave a lot of room for interpretation. They open the manager to challenges about what was meant and why the message was not delivered more clearly. In court, the manager may argue that further explanation was provided during the performance review meeting. The employee may respond that he does not recall that part of the discussion. The jury may use the written performance review to decide whom to believe.

Managers must be taught to use specific examples of performance to make their points about job performance. Specific examples help the manager to draw a clear picture of the employee's performance. They are particularly important when the reviewer is addressing subjective performance expectations such as customer service. For example, a manager might write the following:

> Three customers have complained about the service you provided to them. One indicated that you were rude. When I asked her what she meant by "rude," she told me that you turned your back and walked away from her when she asked you about an extended warranty. When I asked you what had happened with this customer, you told me that you thought she was asking too many questions.

These specific examples make it much easier to support the manager's conclusion that the employee was rude. Examples help the manager to define performance issues in objective terms. They also keep the discussion job related. The performance issues they illustrate are the issues the manager and the employee should spend time discussing.

■ Correcting Performance Problems

Some managers do a good job of defining a performance problem, but they fail to explain specifically what the employee needs to do to correct it. As a result, the employee is able to argue that he or she did not know how to improve performance and get back in the manager's good graces. For example, it is not unusual to see statements like these in a performance review:

> Mary needs to try harder.
>
> Fred needs to do a lot better.
>
> You need to start doing as well as your co-workers do.
>
> You need to improve the quality of your work.

These statements do not tell the employee what to do or how to do it. They show that the manager is frustrated but not that the manager is trying to help the employee correct a problem. General statements like these leave the manager's efforts to coach the employee to success open to a legitimate challenge. Managers must be taught to write clear objectives to help an employee correct a performance problem. A clear objective defines the outcome the employee must provide. It defines the manager's expectations in understandable, achievable, and measurable terms like these:

> We have discussed the importance of customer service. Our standard is to have every customer leave the store feeling that his or her needs were met. To meet this standard, you must greet all customers as they enter the store. You must introduce yourself by name. You must ask them how you can help them. You must listen to their concerns or interests carefully and ask them questions to clarify their needs or interests. You must use your training and the resources available to you in the store to respond to their requests. If you are unable to meet the needs of the customer, you must ask a co-worker or me for help. If our help is not available, you must ask customers if you can call them with an answer as soon as possible. When customers leave the store, you must thank them for visiting.

This objective defines the performance standard (in this case, meet the needs of the customer) and explains what the employee needs to do to achieve it. It provides options if the employee experiences a problem (in this case, manager's unavailability). Most important, it is measurable. The employee's performance can be measured against it by comparing the content of customer feedback.

■ Clarifying Consequences

In many wrongful termination cases, the employee is able to argue that he or she did not know the consequences of failing to perform. Managers must clearly indicate when an employee's continued employment is in jeopardy. The employee cannot be the last one to find out about serious performance concerns.

Again, there should be no surprises in a performance review. If there are performance problems, the employee should be told about them at the time they occur, not months later in the performance review. However, if the problems continue at the time a performance review is due, they should be documented. If the problems are serious enough, they should be accompanied by a clear message that indicates that the employee's continued employment is at risk.

■ Eliminating Discrimination

We would all like to think that discrimination is no longer a workplace issue, but it is. A performance review can be a perfect place to find it. Statements that refer to race, sex, religion, national origin, or other protected categories are inappropriate in a performance review. Some not-so-subtle examples include the following:

> She works just as hard as the guys do.
>
> For a male secretary he does a pretty good job.
>
> Since he returned from drug rehab, he has been here every day.
>
> She tends to talk only to members of her own group. They don't mix with others.

Statements like these are obviously inappropriate in any employment setting, much less in a document that becomes a permanent part of a personnel file. However, there are less obvious ways that a performance review can show bias or a pattern of discrimination.

Retaliation

A performance review can be used to show that a manager has retaliated against an employee for filing a formal complaint. For example, in some cases employees consistently receive ratings above the midpoint for several years. Shortly after they file a discrimination complaint they receive a review with ratings below the midpoint. It is not hard for juries to conclude that the lower ratings appear to be in retaliation for filing the complaint. Unless the managers provide specific, factual examples to show that performance has declined, the employees may be able to argue that there is a connection between the lower rating and the discrimination complaint.

Over-evaluation

Supervisors sometimes give employees a higher rating than they deserve to avoid a conflict. They rate the employee as "satisfactory" instead of "needs improvement" to avoid having to justify their rating to their manager, HR, and the employee. Over time, however, the supervisors tire of the poor performances and decide to terminate the employee. But the reviews do not support the reason given for the termination. If the employee files a legal claim, the inconsistency may be viewed as possible evidence that the employer has given a false reason for termination in order to mask an illegal one, such as discrimination. Reviewers must be trained and held accountable for giving objective evaluations based on job-related criteria.

Close Friendships

Managers are people. They have friends. That is okay unless those friendships affect performance ratings. In some cases, employees can show that their lower ratings seem to be a result of not being involved in the hunting, golfing, shopping, or other outside activities of their manager. It works like this. The managers participate in certain activities with only men or only women or only members of some other group. Since the employees in question are not members of that group, they are not invited or they do not feel comfortable participating and little or no effort is made to help them join in. If an analysis of performance ratings supports their suspicions, they may successfully claim that the reviews document their managers' bias.

Inconsistent Evaluations

Reviewers sometimes hold one employee but not others responsible for doing the job a certain way. Attendance is a good example. Some employees receive negative feedback for being late to work a few times. Others arrive late repeatedly but receive no feedback. Reviewers need to be trained to apply rules and performance standards consistently. It is helpful to have them ask this question: Does the performance issue I am addressing here apply to anyone else? If the answer is yes, the reviewer must be sure to address the problem with the other employees.

Layoffs

Employers often use performance as one of the criteria for selecting employees for layoff or recall. Employees sometimes use performance reviews to demonstrate a bias for or against a protected group being included in the layoff. They use the reviews to show that members of a protected group received lower ratings than those who were retained during the layoff. Managers can prevent such claims by providing specific, factual examples to support their ratings.

■ HR's Responsibilities

The lesson is clear for all managers. Performance reviews must be job related. They must be free of obvious, not-so-obvious, and subtle indications of discrimination and bias. Any unusual or lower-level ratings must be supported by specific examples of performance.

HR plays an important role in preventing performance reviews from becoming legal fodder against the employer. HR needs to watch for rating patterns that may indicate a bias toward or against certain groups. HR needs to monitor review ratings and comments following discrimination or harassment complaints to be sure that they do not indicate attempts to retaliate against the employee. Reviews that contain inappropriate references should be removed from the file and rewritten to include only job-related feedback. Reviewers who write such statements should be retrained and/or disciplined to correct the problem.

Chapter Three:
Implementing an Effective Performance Review System

Designing a performance management system is one thing. Implementing it is another. Careful thought needs to be given to how and when to introduce a new system.

■ Give Advance Notice

It goes without saying that people do not always like change. They often need help to prepare for change, especially when it affects their jobs and potentially their pay. It may take six months to a year to develop a new performance management system. It is important to let managers and employees know that change is in the works. If they find out about the new system just before it is implemented, it will meet with more resistance.

It is also important to invite managers and employees to give input on the design of the new system. Sample forms can be posted on the intranet or bulletin boards. Employees and managers can be asked to comment on the posted drafts. They might just come up with the one idea that is missing to make the system work effectively.

■ Sign Up a Management Champion

If only human resources sees the value in a new performance management program, it will probably fail. If HR teams with a key manager to introduce the new program, it will be much more likely to succeed. The supporting manager does not necessarily have to be the top manager. He or she needs to be a visible manager who will speak up in meetings about the value of effective reviews and the design of the new system.

■ Use an Employee Focus Group

The employee is the primary customer of the performance management system. It is important to ask employees what kind of performance feedback they want. One way to collect this information is to meet with employees in small groups. You can share various approaches, including the sample forms in this book, with them. Their feedback will help you to design a system that meets their needs.

■ Start with a Pilot Project

If time permits, it is very wise to test your new system in one or two departments. It is better to work out the bugs on a small scale than to have to rework the system across the entire organization.

| Figure 5 | Sample Goals for a Performance Appraisal Program |

People Count: Talking about Performance

Our success as an organization depends on productivity. It is important for us to talk about what we do and how we do it to be sure that we are meeting the needs of our customers. Our new People Count performance management system has three goals:

1. To encourage managers and employees to talk about jobs and job performance regularly

2. To allow each individual to contribute as much as possible by providing feedback on what is being done right, what can be done better, and what might be changing for each employee

3. To help employees grow professionally in their role with our organization

---

You have two choices. First, you can introduce the system within a department and tell employees in that department that their reviews will be based on the new system during the pilot project. This approach provides real-time experience with the new process. Second, you can recreate the last review cycle in a department. Under this option, managers are asked to use the new system to recreate the last round of reviews. The advantage of this approach is that it is non-threatening to employees. The reviews and other documents from the pilot project are not placed in their file.

In either approach, it is important to build in an evaluation component. After the pilot, talk with managers and employees to collect their thoughts, perceptions, and feelings about the new system.

■ Have Clear Goals and Honest Answers

More than one HR initiative has failed because the HR professional was unable to explain the purpose and goal of the project. A "sales and marketing plan" that you develop in advance will help introduce the new system. The message that introduces the new system should make sense to managers and employees. It will not work if only the HR team is convinced it is well planned. **Figure 5** is a sample list of goals for a new program.

You also need to be ready to answer some tough questions. Your pilot project should give you an idea as to what those questions will be, but here are a few you will want to think about.

From managers:

When will the new system go into effect?

Will I still be able to use the supplemental form that I developed for my department?

Do I have to fill out every section of the form? What if I think something does not apply to my employee?

Is this project finalized, or is there still room for changes if we find problems when we first use it?

| Figure 6 | Sample Performance Training Goals |

Manager Training

As a result of attending and participating in this program, managers will be able to do the following:

1. Explain and discuss three reasons for doing performance reviews in our organization

2. Work with employees to develop performance goals that are specific, measurable, and realistic

3. Invite, receive, and use employee input as part of planning and writing a performance review

4. Discuss performance feedback with employees in an objective, job-related manner

Employee Training

As a result of attending and participating in this program, employees will be able to do the following:

1. Participate in a discussion with their manager to provide input on their work for their performance review

2. Plan to participate in a two-way discussion with their manager about the feedback in their performance review

3. Provide objective feedback on their experience with the performance review process

---

What is the point of doing reviews if we cannot afford pay increases this year?

From employees:

Will this change the timing or amount of my pay increase?

What happens if I disagree with the comments my manager writes on my review?

This is the third time the review system has been revised in the five years I have been here. How long is this one going to last?

Why do three people sign the review before I see it?

One thing to remember is that regardless of how much time you spend planning, someone will always come up with a question that you did not anticipate. While such questions come late in the process, they can sometimes save an otherwise effective system. It is better to take a little longer to correct flaws than to implement a system with known defects.

■ Offer Training

Most organizations focus on training managers to understand the new system. It is assumed that employees are passive participants in the performance review process. This may be one of the biggest mistakes made in performance management. Employees should be given an opportunity to learn about the system and their role in it. They cannot be effective participants if they do not know how the system works. **Figure 6** shows some potential goals for performance management training.

Your training goals will guide you through planning your program. An effective program will accomplish the following four goals:

■ Introduce participants to an idea, concept, or skill.

■ Let participants experiment with the idea, concept, or skill.

■ Provide helpful feedback on how well participants are using the new idea, concept, or skill.

■ Provide tools for participants to use when they leave the program.

Training Managers

A successful training program for managers includes various elements.

Introduction—The program should start with an overview of what you hope to accomplish and how you plan to accomplish it. List your training goals and briefly explain the types of exercises and activities the group will be involved in.

Caution participants that the class is not the place to talk about specific performance problems. Employee names, current performance issues, and other confidential information should not be mentioned in class discussions.

Opening exercise—It is useful to open the training with an exercise to help the group members get to know one another and to start focusing on performance management. One way to do this is to ask participants to share their own experiences with performance reviews. For example, you might ask half of the room to work in pairs to discuss the most effective review they ever received and the other half to talk about the least effective review they ever received. When the groups are finished sharing, you can ask a few of them to share their stories. You can use their stories to highlight some of the key points you will be covering in class.

Defining jobs, setting goals—There are many ways to organize your session. One easy and logical approach is to follow the path of a new employee. You want the new employee to get a clear picture of what the job is and how the manager expects it to be done. You can start the training process at this point.

For example, you could share some of the experiences that employees shared with you when you were doing your research to illustrate good and bad experiences for new employees. You could then ask the group members to work together to come up with some of their own ideas for introducing new employees into the organization and helping them to learn about their new jobs. Next, you could introduce the process you have developed for new employees. You can refer to the comments and ideas the group suggested to show the similarities between their ideas and your new plans. Finally, you might introduce them to any new forms or procedures related to new employees and give them a case study that allows them to use the forms for an imaginary employee.

Being aware of legal issues—It is important to provide an overview of the legal issues related to performance reviews. Managers do not need to know everything about the law that a labor attorney knows—or even as much as an HR professional knows. They do need to know when they may be in an area that could create problems. And they need to know where to get advice. Your program should give them this information.

Tracking performance during the review period—One of the most important skills you can teach managers is to keep track of key performance events during the year. It is a good idea to spend some time showing managers how to do the following:

- Address key performance issues when they occur.

- Allow employees to explain what they did and why they did it.

- Explain what they want the employee to do in the future.

- Make a note (or keep a sample) of the key performance event and their conversation with the employee.

Writing and presenting the review—Chapter Four provides a detailed discussion about how to prepare a performance review and present it to an employee. You can use the information in this chapter in this section of your class, covering some key points:

- Inviting employee input.

- Using specific examples.

- Writing reviews that use the past to help the employee perform successfully in the future.

- Receiving and considering employee feedback.

Working with the new form—At this point, you can introduce your new form. After you teach managers how to write a review, you can have them work together to complete some or all of your new form to review an imaginary employee.

Following up—Your program can end by showing managers how to follow up on performance issues throughout the year. You will want to give them tips on how to provide positive feedback to employees who meet or exceed their goals for the new review period, how to give constructive feedback to employees who continue to struggle or develop new performance issues, and how to help employees adjust to changes in policy or practice that affect their jobs.

Training Employees

Your training program for employees does not need to be as detailed as the one for managers. It does need to help employees understand their role in the review process. At a minimum, it should include these elements:

Introduction—Start the program by explaining why and how the organization does performance reviews. Let employees know that the organization wants them to be an active part of the process.

Opening exercise—As in the managers' class, it is important to encourage employees to participate as much as possible. An early exercise to get them talking helps break the ice. Unlike in the managers' class, you may not want them to talk about their worst experience with a performance review; that may be opening a Pandora's box. It is better to ask them to pair off to describe a manager who was particularly good at providing feedback. When they are done, ask a few of them to share their stories. Use their stories to highlight some of the points you will be covering in the program.

Providing input—Employees need to be shown how to give input to their managers. They need to learn how to provide specific examples of their performance throughout the year. Most important, they need to know that the organization expects their manager to use their input as part of his or her research to prepare the review.

Clarifying the goals of reviews—You can use this section to help employees understand what their managers are trying to accomplish in the review. It is important for them to understand that their managers will be talking to them about things that are going well, things that need to be corrected, and things that may change. Once you explain the three different goals, you can give them a sample completed performance review and ask them to work together to find each of the three messages in the sample review.

Offering feedback on the process—If your process includes asking employees for feedback on how well the performance review went, they need to learn what type of feedback you want and how to give it. They need help understanding that you want them to share information that tells you whether they thought the reviews were job related and helpful to them in performing their jobs.

Chapter Four:
Planning, Presenting, and Finalizing the Review

The best performance review system in the world easily can be brought to its knees by the way an individual manager delivers a review to an employee. The setting, the conversation, the time of day, and a host of other factors can affect how the review is received.

■ Requesting Employee Input

It is increasingly important to ask for employee input before the review is written or presented. (Please note that giving input is different from doing a self-evaluation. That is discussed below.) In today's world, organizations ask employees to collaborate on a host of projects and assignments every day. The invitation to collaborate should extend to the performance review.

Employees want to be a part of things that affect them, and a performance review definitely affects them. It is a good idea to give them an opportunity to provide input. Inviting input simply means asking the employee to reflect on the many events that occurred during the performance period. It helps the manager to recall and consider the full array of contributions the employee may have made. There are two different ways for employees to give their input, verbally and in writing.

Verbal Input

The employee can be asked to sit down with the manager before the review is written. The manager asks the employee to reflect on the performance period and summarize any highlights that may be important to him. For example:

> Thanks for meeting with me today, Hue. It is time for me to prepare your annual performance review. Before I look through my own notes and samples of your work, I would like to offer you the opportunity to remind me of things that were important to you during the review period. What are some of the things you think about when you reflect on the last year?

The manager should simply listen to what the employee says, asking questions to clarify as necessary. The purpose of this discussion is to give the employee an opportunity to share. It is not to debate or correct the employee's input. The manager should listen carefully, take notes, and repeat significant comments to be sure that the points were understood.

Some employees may be reluctant to offer comments. Their reasons may range from concern about how their manager will react to complex diversity issues about their culture. It may just be that they are shy. The manager should encourage but not require the employee to comment. In the proper setting, the manager, perhaps with the help of an HR professional, may ask the employee to help her understand the employee's reluctance to comment.

If the manager asks for input in this way, it is important for her to refer to it in the performance review. For example, the manager might write something like this in the body of the review:

> Our standard for teamwork is that staff collaborate on key projects by sharing ideas, listening carefully to others to understand their perspective, and working together to solve problems for the benefit of our customers. You are particularly effective at this. When I asked you for your input before writing this review, you reminded me of the efforts your team made on the Beagle project. Several staff commented to me that they enjoyed working with you on that project because you always asked them for their ideas and suggestions. One team member told me that he felt comfortable making suggestions because he knew that no matter how crazy his ideas might be, you would listen to him and treat him and his ideas with respect and dignity. I appreciate your efforts to help and respect others. I encourage you to continue these efforts.

By referring to the employee's input, the manager shows that the input was both heard and valued.

Written Input

The employee can be asked to submit comments in writing. Since this is a work assignment, times should be provided during the workday for non-exempt employees to complete the form. A sample form is shown in Part 2 of this book. The form can be a very helpful tool. However, it should be used carefully. Many employees do not write as a part of their normal job duties. They may find it difficult to express their ideas in writing. If that is the case, the manager could use the form as a guide for interviewing the employee.

It takes time, effort, and energy to complete the form. It is important for the manager to acknowledge the employee's efforts. Managers should be taught to thank the employee for returning the form in person, by telephone, by e-mail, or with a personal note. If possible, the manager should mention at least one specific idea that the employee offered to demonstrate that the employee's input was read and will be considered in writing the review. If the manager takes time to acknowledge the employee, she will be more likely to give input again before the next review period. If the manager does not make that effort, the employee will very likely take longer or not submit the form the following year.

■ Including Self-Evaluation

Some systems ask employees to evaluate their own performances using the same form the manager completes. The manager reviews the completed form and considers it when writing the review. An alternative approach is for the manager to prepare a review without looking at the employee's input. When the employee and the manager meet, first they exchange the forms. They then discuss similarities and differences in their findings and collaborate on a third form that becomes the final review. If this option is used, it is important for the employee to understand that the manager will make the final decision on what will be written on the form, even on points where the two disagree.

■ Using 360-Degree Reviews

In a 360-degree performance review, colleagues, customers, and others comment on the employee's performance during the review period. (Some organizations use 360-degree feedback for career planning and development. Feedback that is collected for developmental purposes should be kept separate from the performance-review process.)

The input for a performance review must be requested well in advance of the review so the manager has time to consider it before writing the review. It is important for those providing input to be trained to provide objective, nondiscriminatory, job-related feedback on actual job duties. A 360-degree review is intended not as a popularity contest but as a way to get a complete picture of how the employee interacts with others while doing his job. (In some states, the law may permit employees to see the comments submitted by the reviewers. Check with a labor attorney in your state before using a 360-degree review or promising confidentiality to reviewers.) A 360-degree review process can be a very effective tool. But implementing it requires an extremely careful planning and design process.

■ Scheduling

It is a good idea to schedule the performance review meeting a few days in advance. The employee should not be surprised to hear about the meeting. The manager should carefully consider the proper time for the meeting. In a hectic environment where people are worn out at the end of the day, it may be best to hold the meeting in the morning. On the other hand, if the manager expects the review to be difficult because of serious performance issues, it may be best to meet at the end of the day, so the employee can go home when it is completed.

The manager needs to decide whether to give the employee a copy of the written review before the meeting. Many managers like to do this because it gives the employee an opportunity to prepare for the discussion. Other managers prefer to discuss the review with the employee before providing a copy. In a sense, they treat the written review as a summary of their discussion with the employee. Either approach can work. What is most important is that the manager and the employee both understand what is being done and why.

■ Attending to the Environment

After an employee performance review workshop, a participant asked the instructor to talk to her supervisor about the environment for giving her a performance review. The conversation went something like this:

> **Participant:** Would you ask my supervisor to get up from her desk and walk over to sit in the chairs in the corner of her office before she gives me my performance review?
>
> **Course leader:** Well, I think you could ask her to do that, but why is it important to you?
>
> **Participant:** Because that is what she does all year. We always sit in the corner chairs to talk about what we need to talk about. One time each year, she stays at her desk when I walk into her office. At that moment, I realize that she is about to give me my annual performance review. It really makes me uncomfortable because it is so different from what we do every other time we meet.

This employee offered some valuable feedback. The place where the meeting is held and the way it is held can make a huge difference in how the employee responds to what the manager has to say. It is a good idea for the manager to ask the employee where he or she would like to meet. It could be the conference room, the manager's office, or even the picnic table under the tree behind the building. The important thing is that the meeting be in a quiet place without interruptions, where both the manager and the employee feel free to share ideas. A restaurant, bar, or hotel room is an inappropriate location for the discussion.

■ Starting the Conversation

If location is important, starting the conversation with the right words is critical. The manager needs to set a positive, constructive, and forward-looking tone from the very beginning. The manager should start the conversation by explaining what the performance review is about and what she hopes to accomplish with it. For example, a manager might say this:

> Thank you for meeting with me today, Rita. As you know, it is time to discuss your annual performance review. We do performance reviews once a year to give us an opportunity look back at how you do your job and how you work with others. It gives us a chance to reflect on how things have been done and talk about how to do them in the future. As we look over the year, we will find things that have been going well, some things that could be done a little bit better, and some things that will be done differently down the road. I want to encourage you to share your ideas and thoughts as we go along. Do you have any questions before we get started?

In other words, it is important for the manager to establish both a purpose and a goal for the meeting.

■ Addressing Performance Contributions

If an employee has done something well, it is important for the manager to acknowledge it. The acknowledgment should be specific, not general:

> **General:** You are really great at writing reports.

Specific: You are really good at writing reports. For example, the report you did on the User's Conference had an easy-to-read and understandable summary of each breakout session. Your tables and charts gave the reader a quick reference and overview of attendance each day and at each conference. I particularly liked the way you used text boxes to highlight key points that will help us have an even better conference next year. I encourage you to continue organizing your reports so they are easy for the reader to understand.

The specifics reinforce what the employee is doing right. By referencing them, the manager demonstrates awareness of what the employee is doing on the job. The reference also sends a message that the manager is pleased with the way the job has been done. It indicates that the employee should keep contributing in the same way in the future.

■ Dealing with Performance Issues

If an employee is not performing well, the manager must discuss the issue in an objective, job-related manner. The manager should start the discussion by explaining the performance standard or expectation:

We expect a customer service representative with your level of experience to handle at least forty-seven calls per day with an average of less than two callbacks or complaints each day.

Starting with the standard sends a message that the conversation is about doing the job, not about the individual. Next, the manager should reference the previous conversations on the topic:

We have talked about your call volume three times this year. In January, we discussed . . .

Referencing the past discussions reminds the employee that the manager has been working to correct the problem throughout the year. Next, the manager should bring the employee up to date on any issues that have occurred since their last discussion. It is important for the manager to invite the employee to agree or disagree with his or her concerns about the employee's performance. If the employee disagrees, it is important for the manager to listen carefully to why he or she disagrees and then to make an effort to help the employee understand why the problem exists and why the manager is concerned about it.

The next step is to establish an expectation for the employee's future performance. If the standard is established and cannot be varied (in the example above, at least forty-seven calls per day with an average of less than two callbacks or complaints each day), then the manager must explain that it must be met. If the standard is open to discussion, the manager can collaborate with the employee to define it. In the end, the manager must clearly state the performance expectation that he has for the employee.

It is a good idea for the manager to suggest tools that might help the employee to meet the performance expectation. For example, the manager might suggest going to training, consulting with a more experienced employee, or looking at a book or catalog before taking a particular action. It would be very appropriate for the manager to ask the employee for any other ideas of what would help him meet the performance standard. For example, in one case when a manager asked one employee what he thought would help him get to work on time, he answered, "I don't know. I guess maybe I could buy an alarm clock." It may seem silly, but asking the question brought out a problem that had not been discussed and provided a way for the manager to reinforce that the employee needed to solve the problem.

The final step in discussing a performance issue is letting the employee know how serious the matter is. If it is a minor issue, the manager needs only to let the employee know that he or she will check periodically to see if the problem is corrected. If it is a serious problem, the manager must tell the employee that failure to correct it will have negative consequences for their continued employment.

■ Ending the Conversation

The conversation should end where it started. At the beginning of the meeting, the manager indicated that the overall goal was to look at the past year to help the employee understand what to do in the future. As a result, the manager should summarize the future performance expectations she has for the employee. The summary should include reinforcing performance behaviors the manager would like the employee to keep doing, restating which performance behaviors need to be corrected, and explaining any new or different duties that may be assigned to the employee during the coming performance review period.

■ Soliciting Employee Feedback

Most systems invite the employee to provide feedback at the end of the performance review process. The purpose of this feedback is twofold. First, it gives the employee an opportunity to ask questions that may not have been answered in the conversation or in the written review. Second, it helps the manager to see if the employee received the intended messages.

It is a good idea to give the employee time to think about feedback. Some managers ask the employee to fill out the feedback section of the review form at the end of the performance review meeting. In most cases, the employee writes "no comment," signs the form, and gives it back to the manager. This usually means the employee is still absorbing the array of information the manager has provided and is not prepared to offer any specific comments.

A better approach is to give the employee a copy of the review and ask her to read it over again and reflect on the conversation in the meeting. The employee should be invited to come back a few days later and note comments on the original form. The manager should take time to review the employee's comments. If they reveal any concerns or questions, it may be appropriate to schedule a second meeting.

■ Considering Other Issues

In the process of preparing the review and meeting with the employee, some other issues may need to be considered, including the following.

Performance Reviews and Salary

Some organizations tie performance reviews and salary together. If the employee is eligible for an increase, it is given at the same time as the review. Other organizations do the review at one time and grant the increase at another. Regardless of which approach is used, the most important issue is that the manager and the employee both understand how the system works. Despite all the theory about separating performance reviews and pay, most employees come to the performance review thinking that the two are linked. The manager must be able to explain the link or the lack of it in clear, understandable terms.

Understanding *versus* Agreeing

We live in a world of sharing and collaboration. A performance review presents an interesting paradox in that environment. While we invite employees to participate in the process, when it comes to evaluating overall job performance, the boss still has to be the boss. Someone has to decide how things are going and where they should go. That responsibility falls on the manager. The discussion of the performance review does not always have to result in agreement, but it does have to result in understanding.

In other words, the employee may not agree with the manager's performance standards or evaluation. He or she must, however, be given a reasonable opportunity to understand them. For example, in one situation a manager wanted employees to state their name as part of their greeting when they answered the phone. One employee objected to saying her name until she knew who was calling. The manager could not get her to agree that she should say her name. As a result, the manager had to change the tone of the conversation to help her understand that she was expected to state her name. She did not like the policy, but she left the performance discussion understanding that she was expected to follow it.

Discontinued Projects

If an employee starts a project but does not finish it because of a change in business direction or priorities, the manager should give the employee credit for his efforts in the beginning stages of the assignment. It is likely that other projects will be discontinued in the future, so it is important for the manager to show appreciation for the employee's efforts to start or even complete the discontinued project.

Chapter Five:
After the Review

The most important part of a review is what happens when it is all done. In fact, the review is the starting point, not the ending point. It records what has occurred with the most important purpose of providing direction for the future. After the review, the manager must follow up with the employee to ensure that the goals it included are met. The manager must provide ongoing feedback to guide the employee's continued progress.

■ Follow Up on Effective Employee Contributions

Managers sometimes take the contributions of an above-average contributor for granted. Attendance is a good example. Most people with perfect attendance will tell you that their manager has never acknowledged their record. They will tell you that they feel slighted. Managers must be trained to recognize and reward all performance that helps the organization to meet its objectives.

To encourage employees who are meeting or exceeding performance standards, a manager should constantly work to provide feedback that is timely and ongoing, specific, and sincere.

Timely, Ongoing Feedback

The manager should watch for opportunities to reinforce effective employee contributions. This does not mean complimenting every contribution every time. It does mean that when a manager observes a behavior that contributes to the mission of the organization, he should find a way to reinforce it with the employee. For example, on one hot summer day in a manufacturing facility, a supervisor noticed that one employee wore her hardhat and safety glasses all day long. Many other workers ignored the rule that day because perspiration was causing the glasses to slip down their noses and the hats to slide around on their heads. The manager pulled the employee aside and quietly said:

> Thanks for wearing your safety glasses and your hard hat on a day like this. I know it can be a real pain, but those things are designed to keep us safe so we can go home in one piece at night. I really appreciate your following the policy.

The same kinds of comments can be made about reports, projects, customer service, and virtually any other employee contribution. When a manager reinforces an employee's contributions on an ongoing basis, the employee is more likely to continue making those contributions.

One interesting mistake that managers make is waiting for big events to occur before recognizing employee contributions. In most organizations, the worker mentioned in the last example would have to wait for the annual safety award meeting to hear about her manager's appreciation. This is a mistake. Great performance does not result from annual recognition. (Imagine starring in a Broadway play where the audience is allowed to applaud only once each year.) Great performance results from being involved in how the job is done and receiving regular feedback on contributions.

Another mistake managers make when they talk to a successful employee is talking too much. Employees know when they are doing a good job or putting forth extra effort. They want their manager to recognize it. If you give *them* a chance to talk about it you will learn a lot more about what they are doing and they will be more committed to doing it. Managers need to learn to use magical words like these:

> This looks like a really nice job. What did you do to make it turn out so well?

Managers who listen carefully to the answer build credibility with employees and become significantly more knowledgeable about what it takes to succeed in the organization.

Specific Feedback

General feedback is rarely effective. It may sound good. It may feel positive, but it does little to help an employee move successfully into the future. If specific feedback is important in the performance review, it is even more important during the review period.

> **General:** That's great. I wish we had more people with your drive and initiative.
>
> **Specific:** Bob at the Lamp Company called to tell me that you solved the custom design problem. He said that he was really impressed that you drove over there and studied the plans and came back here to work with our engineers. He told me you were over there till midnight two nights last week. I really appreciate it when you take the initiative to understand our customers' needs and work hard to help them. Can you tell me a little more about what you did?

Specific feedback both reinforces desired behaviors and motivates the employee to repeat them.

Sincere Feedback

Once in a while, a manager hears a motivational speaker say that he/she should give employees lots of feedback and encouragement. Managers walk in the next morning telling everyone what a great job they are doing and to keep up the good work. By the time the managers get to their desks, employees are betting on which political office the managers are running for.

Effective feedback must come from the heart, not from a book or a speech. It needs to be sincere. If the manager does not believe it, she should not say it. If she does say it, it should be expressed sincerely.

Different managers give sincere feedback in different ways. Some do it in front of groups. Some do it with a handwritten note. The style is not as important as the fact that the employee thinks and feels that the manager believes it.

■ Follow Up on Areas Where Improvement Is Needed

When a performance review identifies areas where improvement is needed, the manager must redouble his efforts to create an opportunity for the employee to succeed. In too many cases, when a poor performer leaves the performance review meeting, the manager wipes the sweat from his brow, takes a deep breath, and hopes that there will not be a need for a follow-up meeting. They are usually wrong. Their failure to plan for that meeting and subsequent meetings often leads to an even more difficult situation.

When an employee's performance review indicates that improvement is needed, the manager must be careful to follow up in subsequent weeks and months.

Watch for Small Indicators of Improvement

Performance problems do not usually start overnight, and they are rarely corrected overnight. If the performance review is written and discussed correctly, the employee should understand what needs to be done to correct the problem. The manager should carefully watch for any sign of improvement. Progress usually is not made in large steps; it is made through many small steps. The manager should reinforce those steps whenever it will help the employee to keep moving in the right direction. Keep in mind that it may not be appropriate to comment on every little improvement.

Keep Matters Confidential

It goes without saying that performance issues should be dealt with confidentially. Unfortunately, performance problems are great fodder for water cooler discussions. Managers sometimes forget the importance of helping an employee who is struggling to maintain dignity by keeping the issues as confidential as possible. In most cases, discussion should be limited to the manager, her manager, human resources (HR), and legal counsel; the problem really should not go beyond that.

Make Sure Feedback Is Timely and Specific

When problems do occur, the manager must address them as soon as it is practical to do so. Specific examples of the performance problem must be used to help the employee understand why the manager continues to be concerned. It is important for the manager to carefully consider why the problem continues to be a problem. Employees do not usually do things wrong on purpose. Many times they do what they think is right at the time, based upon their previous experiences and knowledge. The manager's job is to make sure the employee knows about and knows how to use all of the possible alternative ways to do the job.

Encourage Employee Participation

Employees usually will do what they are told—if they feel they must. However, if the manager really wants the employee to solve the problem, he needs to find a way to involve the employee in designing the solution. Here's an example:

> Manesha, we have talked about the importance of checking input screens before you log off of them. You know that our standard is 98 percent accuracy. The reports show that you have had an 85 percent accuracy rating for the last three weeks. I really need you to fix this problem. What do you think you can do to get to the 98 percent level?

The manager should encourage the employee to offer several suggestions. The manager should then work with the employee to evaluate each alternative, select the one that is most likely to succeed, and encourage the employee to use it. If it solves the problem, the manager should acknowledge the progress. If it does not, the manager may need to consult with HR and legal counsel to implement corrective action or termination.

Make the Tough Decisions

No one likes to fire an employee. But if all efforts to correct a performance problem fail, the manager must be prepared to make a final decision about continued employment. If termination is being considered, an independent third party (HR, labor attorney) should help the manager review the case. Many factors must be considered in a termination decision. Generally, however, if no legal hurdles are present (for instance, discrimination, implied contracts, etc.) and the independent review shows that the employee was properly trained and given a fair opportunity to correct the problem, it may be in the best interests of the employee and the employer to end the employment relationship.

■ Follow Up on New Procedures and Processes

Very often, jobs change as a result of new equipment, new programs, or other legitimate business changes. If these changes are known at the time of the performance review, they should be discussed with the employee. As a part of the review and in the weeks and months following it, the manager should do the following.

Explain the Change

Regardless of the source or the reason, a change in the way an employee is expected to do a job can be unsettling. Such change is always easier to accept if the manager makes an effort to help the employee understand it and why it came about. The employee does not necessarily have to agree that the change is necessary, but an explanation can encourage understanding and acceptance.

Explain the Impact

Once the need for the change is explained, the next question the employee will ask is, How does it affect me? The manager needs to establish clear performance expectations that tell the employee what he needs to do to adjust to the change. The manager should engage in a dialogue with the employee to determine the best ways to bring about the desired change.

Offer Help or Assistance

Change often brings uncertainty. It involves trying new things and making mistakes. An important part of bringing about change is helping employees through the process. The manager should offer support and assistance to help the employee adjust to the new way of doing things.

Acknowledge Progress

As the change process unfolds, it is important for the manager to acknowledge the employee's progress. If the employee is successfully navigating the change, the manager should follow the steps discussed in the "Follow Up on Effective Employee Contributions" section above. If the employee does not adjust, the manager should apply the steps in the "Follow Up on Areas Where Improvement Is Needed" section.

Part 2:
Sample Forms

The sample forms in this section have been contributed by organizations that have developed them for use with their own specific performance appraisal systems. Before using or adapting any performance appraisal form, you should have the form reviewed by your organization's legal counsel.

Information, such as a company name, that identified the contributing organization has been removed from each form. When this information was in the body of the form, a phrase in brackets [] has been substituted. For example, "ABC Company" has been changed to [Company]. In adapting any of the forms, you can substitute your organization's individual information for the bracketed material.

The sample forms are in electronic files on the accompanying CD-ROM. They are in two formats: Portable Document Format and Rich Text Format. See "Using the Accompanying CD-ROM" at the back of the book for more information about these files.

A. Introductory Period Reviews

An employee's first few weeks and months on the job are critical. During this time, an employee learns about the job, the supervisor, the co-workers, and the new employer. Feedback is never more important than when a person is learning.

1. **Six-month Performance Appraisal:** Offers a complete review; labeled for use with new employees, page 45

2. **Orientation Period Performance Appraisal Form:** Provides minimal job trait categories, page 47

3. **Employee 90 Day Review:** Uses a check-the-box format, page 49

Six-month Performance Appraisal

Date:_____

Employee's Name: _____

Employee's Position: _____

Supervisor's Name: _____

Performance Objectives and Results:

Appraisal Period Goals/Objectives: _____

_____

_____

Performance Versus Goals/Objectives: _____

_____

_____

Other Significant Accomplishments:_____

_____

_____

3-6 Performance Goals/Objectives for Next Appraisal Period: _____

_____

_____

Other Comments: _____

_____

_____

_____

Employee Comments:_____

_____

_____

_____

Please Note: In signing this form, the employee acknowledges only that the appraisal has been reviewed by him/her. Signature does not imply that the employee concurs with this appraisal in whole or in part.

Employee:_____   Date: _____

Supervisor:_____

Human Resources:_____

Orientation Period Performance Appraisal Form

Appraisal Period (90 days from date of hire): _____

Associate Name: _____   Position: _____

Department/Team: _____   Location: _____

Appraising Supervisor/Manager: _____

❏ 30 Day Review   ❏ 60 Day Review   ❏ 90 Day Review

Ratings: 5 - Outstanding
4 - Exceeds Requirements
3 - Meets Requirements
2 - Needs Improvement
1 - Unsatisfactory

Attendance/Punctuality: Rating: _____

Consistently meets standards for attendance and punctuality.

_____

_____

_____

_____

Job Knowledge/Productivity: Rating: _____

Associate demonstrates knowledge of job duties and meets standards for time in the position. Volume of work regularly produced meets standards for time in position.

_____

_____

_____

_____

Communication: Rating: _____

Associate demonstrates ability to interact in a clear and logical manner verbally and in written correspondence. Demonstrates ability to communicate with internal and external clients.

_____

_____

_____

_____

Cooperation & Teamwork: **Rating:** _____

Associate demonstrates willingness to work with and assist others.

_____

_____

_____

_____

Associate Comments:

_____

_____

_____

_____

_____

_____

_____

_____

_____

Associate Signature: _____   Date: _____

Supervisor/Manager Signature: _____   Date: _____

Employee 90 Day Review

Employee Name: _____   Date: _____

Department: _____   Period of Review: _____

Reviewer: _____

Reviewer's Title: _____

	Exceeds Requirements	Meets Requirements	Needs Attention	No Basis
Technical Skills (requisite knowledge to perform job requirements)	❑	❑	❑	❑
Productivity (produces appropriate quantity of error free work)	❑	❑	❑	❑
Organizational Skills (maintains/improves files and information to allow quick retrieval)	❑	❑	❑	❑
Prioritization (performs tasks in order of importance)	❑	❑	❑	❑
Follow Through (attends to task from inception to final resolution)	❑	❑	❑	❑
Accountability (accepts personal responsibility for assigned work)	❑	❑	❑	❑
Innovation (seeks better alternatives for performing assigned tasks)	❑	❑	❑	❑
Problem Solving (manages daily problems independently and efficiently)	❑	❑	❑	❑
Change Management (supports new ideas and exercises flexibility as changes are initiated)	❑	❑	❑	❑
Cooperation (works with others to achieve growth/improvement of department)	❑	❑	❑	❑
Positive Attitude (helps to create an effective work environment)	❑	❑	❑	❑
Pro-active (offers ideas to improve & minimize problems)	❑	❑	❑	❑
Confidentiality (discusses sensitive matters only when appropriate)	❑	❑	❑	❑
Attendance	❑	❑	❑	❑

Employment Recommendation: ❑ Retain   ❑ Extend Introductory Period   ❑ Do Not Retain

Comments: _____

_____

_____

_____

Employee's Signature: _____

Reviewer's Signature: _____

B. Employee Input to Reviews

Some organizations invite employees to provide input to their supervisor on their own job performance. It is important to be sure that the supervisor uses the input as input and not as the final review. It is also important for the supervisor to acknowledge the employee's input during the review process. Generally, the input is requested in one of two ways. The first is to ask the employee to do a self evaluation. The second is to ask the employee for input to help the supervisor address the most important events during the review period.

1. **Employee Self Evaluation Form:** Asks the employee to summarize the job, evaluate the supervisor's communication style, offer insights into career aspirations, list barriers to good performance, and make recommendations for the organization, page 53

2. **Self-Assessment Worksheet:** Asks the employee to focus on one to three general results or broad objectives to assess her contributions during the year, page 55

3. **[Staff Member] Questionnaire:** Asks the member (employee) to assess his performance through a series of self-analysis questions, page 57

4. **Performance Self Assessment:** Asks the employee to self-rate in a variety of categories and provide examples of contributions and areas for development, page 59

Employee Self Evaluation Form

To be completed by the employee

Name _____   Job Title _____

Business Unit Name _____   Cost Center Number _____

Supervisor Name _____

Summarize the tasks and/or responsibilities you have been assigned to perform and include your self-assessment.

List the tasks and/or job responsibilities you have been assigned to perform. This list may also be your objectives for the year. List them in order of impor-tance. Under each, evaluate yourself on your performance on each task/responsibility. Include a description of the following that apply: Did you complete the task? Did you achieve the expected/desired result? Did you complete it in the time frame expected? How well did you communicate the results? How could you have improved? What would you do differently next time? What additional assistance could you have used from your supervisor? What additional tools? Use additional paper if needed.

Tasks/Responsibilities or Objectives	Self Assessment
_____	_____
_____	_____
_____	_____
_____	_____

Communications:

Comment on your supervisor's communication with you. Include comments about: Has your supervisor communicated with you about expected perform-ance results, business information, general company information, company procedures, or policies? What additional information would you like to hear about? From your Department Head? From Human Resources? From _____ or _____ or [Company Officials]? How often?

_____

_____

_____

_____

Career Recommendations:

In this section, discuss the recommendations you have for yourself. Include comments about: your personal career goals, on-the-job training, new chal-lenges/responsibilities you would be interested in, other formal classes or seminars of interest, tools and/or resources needed to improve your performance on the job and to improve your opportunities for career development.

_____

_____

_____

_____

Performance Inhibitors?

What obstacles are in the way of your achieving your performance objectives? What are you planning to do to ensure accomplishment? What actions should your supervisor or the company take to help eliminate these inhibitors?

_____

_____

_____

Recommendations for improvement to the company:

What would you like to see changed in the company?_____

_____

Do you understand the changes taking place as part of our Total Quality Management initiatives?_____

_____

Do you understand the [Company Objectives]? _____

_____

Do you have any ideas about new products or market applications for our products? _____

_____

Do you have suggestions for Process Improvement? _____

_____

Do you have suggestions for how can we improve our service to our customer? _____

_____

Do you feel "Empowered"? ❑ Yes   ❑ No

If no, share your ideas about how your supervisor could or should "Empower" you. _____

_____

Please share your ideas with us here._____

_____

_____

_____

Signature: _____

      Employee   Date

Return this completed form to your Supervisor prior to your formal performance evaluation discussion.
This form should be used as a basis for this discussion.

Self-Assessment Worksheet

Performance Planning

List between one and three general results or broad objectives that you are responsible for.

_____

_____

_____

_____

_____

_____

Specifically, what must you do to accomplish these results or objectives?

_____

_____

_____

_____

_____

_____

What skills, attitudes and behaviors are critical to achieving success in your role?

_____

_____

_____

_____

_____

_____

Self-Evaluation

Explain how you achieved your responsibilities and goals this year.

_____

_____

_____

_____

_____

_____

What challenges made it difficult to meet the performance expectations?

_____

_____

_____

_____

_____

_____

_____

How did your skills, attitudes and behaviors contribute to success in your role?

_____

_____

_____

_____

_____

_____

_____

[Staff Member] Questionnaire

Staff Member: _____

Position: _____ Date: _____

[Staff Member] Objectives	Not Very Effective					Very Effective	N/A Don't Know
[Customer Success]: Do I focus my efforts on helping or serving the customer? Customers may be [Staff Members], outside vendors, and external customers.	❏	❏	❏	❏	❏	❏	❏
[Staff Member] Development: Am I committed to learning, developing, and using new skills?	❏	❏	❏	❏	❏	❏	❏
Teamwork: Do my actions support a complete team environment?	❏	❏	❏	❏	❏	❏	❏
Job Knowledge: Do I possess the skills and knowledge needed to properly perform my job?	❏	❏	❏	❏	❏	❏	❏
100% Measures: Do I understand and work toward the achievement of the 100% Measures?	❏	❏	❏	❏	❏	❏	❏
Innovation and Continuous Improvement: Do I improve individual and team performance by doing new things and making things better?	❏	❏	❏	❏	❏	❏	❏
Problem Solving: Do I participate in identifying problems and offering solutions?	❏	❏	❏	❏	❏	❏	❏
Communication:							
❏ Do I treat peers with respect and dignity?	❏	❏	❏	❏	❏	❏	❏
❏ Do I communicate openly and honestly with my Coach?	❏	❏	❏	❏	❏	❏	❏
❏ Do I take ownership and share in the responsibility of building teamwork through communication with **all** [Staff Members]?	❏	❏	❏	❏	❏	❏	❏
❏ Do I listen attentively and respond in a timely and appropriate manner?	❏	❏	❏	❏	❏	❏	❏
Safety/Compliance: Do I follow Company and Regulatory guidelines and policies?							
❏ Equipment	❏	❏	❏	❏	❏	❏	❏
❏ Human	❏	❏	❏	❏	❏	❏	❏
❏ OSHA	❏	❏	❏	❏	❏	❏	❏
❏ DOT	❏	❏	❏	❏	❏	❏	❏
❏ Product	❏	❏	❏	❏	❏	❏	❏
Attendance: Do I make a commitment to my team by being at work, on-time, and without excessive breaks and personal visiting?	❏	❏	❏	❏	❏	❏	❏
Best Place to Work: Do my actions and attitude promote the Best Place to Work for People Who Want to Become Great?	❏	❏	❏	❏	❏	❏	❏
Other:	❏	❏	❏	❏	❏	❏	❏

Other Comments: _____

_____

_____

_____

List up to two (2) areas in the company that you are/may be interested in working or learning more about. This may include your current department/team.

(1) _____

(2) _____

Strengths: Which of my talents is most helpful in my position and to my team? Please provide a brief example(s). _____

_____

_____

_____

Growth Opportunity: Which skill or behavior, if developed or strengthened, would be most helpful to my team? _____

_____

_____

_____

Performance Self Assessment

Confidential

Employee Name: _____   Position: _____

Department: _____   Supervisor Name: _____

Date Review Due: _____   Date Review Conducted: _____

A. Performance/Competency Self Assessment

Instructions: Rate yourself on the core competency listed below. If the competency is critical to the job, please <u>underline</u> it. If competency listed is not applicable to your position, please mark "n/a."

Rating Definitions

1	Expert	Employee demonstrates competency that is always superior to the job expectation. He/she is considered exceptional among his/her peers.
2	Above Average	Employee demonstrates competency that is consistently above what would be expected for employees at this level.
3	Competent	Employee demonstrates competency at a level that consistently meets and sometimes exceeds the job expectations.
4	Needs Development	Employee needs to develop competency for continued success. Competency is a requirement in the current position in order to progress to next level.
5	Not Demonstrated	Employee does not demonstrate competency. Developmental plan needs to be established in order to provide platforms for demonstrating the competency.

Core Competencies/Skills *Please <u>underline</u> critical skills*	1	2	3	4	5	n/a	**Key Contributions/Areas of Development** *(add examples, as applicable, to clarify rating)*
Verbal communication							
Written communication							
Thinking clearly and analytically							
Creativity, offers new ideas							
Identifying and solving problems							
Initiative							
Time management and prioritization							
Organization							
Flexibility							
Responsibility							
Customer service (internal/external)							
Attention to detail							
Results oriented							
Financial management							
Leadership							
Ability to teach others							
Ability to learn							
Ability to work independently							
PC proficiency							

Employee Name: _____   **Position:** _____

Department: _____   **Supervisor Name:** _____

A. Performance/Competency Self Assessment – Management Competencies

Instructions: If you are a manager of staff, rate yourself on the core competencies listed below. All of the below competencies are deemed *critical leadership skills* and all must be rated. **If you are not a manager of staff, this section should not be completed.**

Rating Definitions

1	Expert	Employee demonstrates competency that is always superior to the job expectation. He/she is considered exceptional among his/her peers.
2	Above Average	Employee demonstrates competency that is consistently above what would be expected for employees at this level.
3	Competent	Employee demonstrates competency at a level that consistently meets and sometimes exceeds the job expectations.
4	Needs Development	Employee needs to develop competency for continued success. Competency is a requirement in the current position in order to progress to next level.
5	Not Demonstrated	Employee does not demonstrate competency. Developmental plan needs to be established in order to provide platforms for demonstrating the competency.

Core Management Competencies/Skills *All below are critical skills*	1	2	3	4	5	n/a	**Key Contributions/Areas of Development** *(add examples, as applicable, to clarify rating)*
Ability to motivate							
Ability/willingness to communicate to staff							
Accountability							
Coaching, mentoring							
Decisiveness							
Delegation ability							
Entrepreneurship							
Performance assessment							
Respect for others							
Staff retention							
Staff selection							
Strategic planning							
Vision							

Employee Name: _____   **Position:** _____

Department: _____   **Supervisor Name:**_____

B. Overall Self Assessment

The overall assessment represents a summary of your evaluation of your demonstrated skills and achievements. Describe in a short summary your contribution to the company; greatest strengths; areas needing improvement; or avenues of potential development.

List Key Contributions/Achievements   **List Areas of Potential Development**

_____   _____

_____   _____

_____   _____

_____   _____

_____   _____

_____   _____

_____   _____

Overall Comments _____

_____

_____

_____

_____

_____

_____

Employee's Signature _____   Date _____

Employee Name:_____   Position: _____

Department: _____   Supervisor Name: _____

C. Midyear Reviews

Most organizations have an annual review period. If you are an employee, twelve months is a long time to wait for feedback. If you are a supervisor, less than twelve months is too soon to have to write a full review again. Some organizations provide an interim review that is usually shorter and more informal than the comprehensive annual review.

1. **Interim Employee Performance Review:** Provides space to summarize progress toward goals and areas for improvement, page 65

2. **Annual Review and Objectives—Production/ Manufacturing:** Provides space for both quarterly feedback and an overall annual review, page 67

Interim Employee Performance Review

Employee Name: _____

Reviewed By: _____   Date: _____

I. Progress on Goals/Objectives

Briefly discuss employee's progress on goals/objectives as identified at the start of the year. Identify any mid year changes to goals and objectives:

_____

_____

_____

II. Areas of Needed Improvement

Note to Reviewing Manager: After considering the action plans, performance objectives, and performance measures not accomplished by the employee, describe the job experience, exposure, and/or training you plan for the employee to improve performance in the current position.

Describe Areas of Needed Improvement: _____

_____

_____

_____

Activities Planned to Improve Performance: _____

_____

_____

_____

Timing:_____

_____

Employee's Comments: _____

_____

_____

_____

We have met and discussed the interim review.

Employee Name:_____   **Manager:** _____

Employee Signature _____   **Date:** _____

Manager Signature_____   **Date:** _____

Annual Review and Objectives – Production/Manufacturing

Employee's Name: _____

Department: _____

Rating Period: *From* _____ ***To*** _____

4 - Outstanding Performance   **2 -** Satisfactory Performance/Meets Expectations   **0 -** Unacceptable Performance/Far-Below Expectations

3 - Performance Exceeds Expectations   **1 -** Performance Below Expectations

Attitude	Quarter 1	Quarter 2	Quarter 3	Quarter 4	Year
Conducts self in a manner that is professional, courteous, and consistent with all company policy, including not speaking negatively about the company, co-workers, supervisors, or others.					
Understands his/her performance directly affects the level of sales and customer satisfaction, and strives to perform so that both continue to increase. Remains positive when changes are made to procedures, routine, environment, and/or responsibilities, and demonstrates this by cooperating and adhering to the changes.					

Comments

Quarter 1 _____

_____

Quarter 2 _____

_____

Quarter 3 _____

_____

Quarter 4 _____

_____

Quality	Quarter 1	Quarter 2	Quarter 3	Quarter 4	Year
Focuses on the smallest of details and always double checks work before submitting it as completed or routing it to the next department.					
Follows the procedures for each job and asks for help if unsure about procedures prior to beginning the job.					
Reports to the Teamleader and/or Supervisor if two consecutive products he/she produces must be placed in second quality or thrown away.					

Comments

Quarter 1 _____

_____

Quarter 2 _____

_____

Quarter 3 _____

_____

Quarter 4 _____

_____

Teamwork/Cooperation

	Quarter 1	Quarter 2	Quarter 3	Quarter 4	Year
Contributes to establishing a work environment that is comfortable for all co-workers by willingly cooperating with all co-workers and treating all co-workers with respect and dignity.					
Provides co-workers with accurate, appropriate feedback when given the opportunity. Resolves disputes directly and appropriately.					
Willingly changes focus from one area to another that has been given priority and focuses on tasks outside of his/her normal responsibilities when needed.					

Comments

Quarter 1 _____

_____

Quarter 2 _____

_____

Quarter 3 _____

_____

Quarter 4 _____

_____

Initiative/Self-Motivation

	Quarter 1	Quarter 2	Quarter 3	Quarter 4	Year
Accepts feedback from quarterly evaluations and does his/her best to apply this feedback to his/her behavior. Seeks knowledge that will provide individual with skills that enable improved job performance and the ability to complete a varied number of products. Identifies areas within department (such as procedures or departmental organization) that need improvement, suggests the improvement, and works to help implement the improvement. Volunteers to complete miscellaneous tasks within his/her department.					

Comments

Quarter 1 _____

_____

Quarter 2 _____

_____

Quarter 3 _____

_____

Quarter 4 _____

_____

Productivity/Quantity of Work

	Quarter 1	Quarter 2	Quarter 3	Quarter 4	Year
Strives to increase the amount that he/she produces, while maintaining a high level of quality. Stays focused and uses time to best benefit. Prioritizes work appropriately.					
Overall output					

Comments

Quarter 1 _____

_____

Quarter 2 _____

_____

Quarter 3 _____

_____

Quarter 4 _____

_____

Safety

	Quarter 1	Quarter 2	Quarter 3	Quarter 4	Year
Works safely, reports safety hazards, and makes suggestions to improve safety.					
Does not engage in horseplay or carelessness. Ensures tools are used in the manner for which they were designed. Encourages co-workers to wear Personal Protective Equipment and work safely.					
Wears Personal Protective Equipment when necessary.					

Comments

Quarter 1 _____

_____

Quarter 2 _____

_____

Quarter 3 _____

_____

Quarter 4 _____

_____

Dependability/Trustworthiness

	Quarter 1	Quarter 2	Quarter 3	Quarter 4	Year
Follows directions given to him/her correctly. Can be trusted to stay in work area and to be focused on work given to him/her. Does not need to be reminded how work is to be done, including processes, format, etc.					

Comments

Quarter 1 _____

_____

Quarter 2 _____

_____

Quarter 3 _____

_____

Quarter 4 _____

_____

Communication

	Quarter 1	Quarter 2	Quarter 3	Quarter 4	Year
Informs direct supervisor and other appropriate individuals regarding problems with co-workers, product, processes, or other things. Speaks and/or writes in a manner so that messages are clear.					

Comments

Quarter 1 _____

_____

Quarter 2 _____

_____

Quarter 3 _____

_____

Quarter 4 _____

_____

Organization

	Quarter 1	Quarter 2	Quarter 3	Quarter 4	Year
Returns items to their proper location, ensuring co-workers will be able to find and access the items. Department and individual workspace is kept clean, organized, and free of unnecessary clutter.					

Comments

Quarter 1 _____

_____

Quarter 2 _____

_____

Quarter 3 _____

_____

Quarter 4 _____

_____

Average Score – Current Quarter

Number of:						
"4's"	"3's"	"2's"	"1's"	"0's"		
x4 =	x3 =	x2 =	x1 =	x0 =	Total	*Final Score*
+	+	+	+	=		Divided by 17 =

Average Score – Year-to-Date

Final Score				
Quarter 1	Quarter 2	Quarter 3	Quarter 4	Average

Punctuality

	Quarter 1	Quarter 2	Quarter 3	Quarter 4
Amount of vacation time used during:				
Amount of sick time used during:				
Amount of time off without pay during:				

Comments

_____

_____

_____

_____

Objectives for Quarter

Personal Performance Objectives for:

Quarter 1 _____

_____

Quarter 2 _____

_____

Quarter 3 _____

_____

Quarter 4 _____

_____

Summary

Summary of Review:

Quarter 1 _____

_____

Quarter 2 _____

_____

Quarter 3 _____

_____

Quarter 4 _____

_____

Your signature indicates that a conference was held on _____ and that you understand your strengths and the importance of their continuation as well as the areas where we wish you to concentrate on improving your performance.

Employee_____   Supervisor_____

Employee Comments/Questions/Concerns/Suggestions:

_____

_____

_____

_____

_____

_____

_____

D. Job Trait or Competence-Based Reviews

Certain basic traits, behaviors, and competencies are part of every job. Some organizations build their review process around these traits. This one-size-fits-all approach provides a form for virtually every job. However, it can lead to very general feedback to the employee, as the supervisor tries to match a generic category like "Quality" to a specific job.

1. **Performance Appraisal Form:** Calls job traits "performance criteria" and provides space for performance feedback, future development, and rating, page 75

2. **Employee Performance Appraisal:** Weighs generic job trait categories and provides limited space for narrative comments, page 81

3. **Employee Performance Review:** Lists job traits and asks both the supervisor and the employee to check a rating and provide comments, page 85

4. **Performance Appraisal—Non-Exempt:** Allows a separate performance rating for each job trait, page 89

5. **Employee Performance Appraisal:** Provides a numerical rating with overall rating and space for narrative comments about strengths and areas for improvement, page 93

Performance Appraisal Form

Appraisal Period: From _____ To _____

Associate Name: _____ Position: _____

Department/Team: _____ Location: _____

Appraising Supervisor/Manager: _____

Dates in Present Position: _____

Performance Appraisal Rating Explanations

5 - Outstanding   Performance and quality of work **far exceeds** what is reasonably expected throughout the entire review period. Assigning this rating should be an exceptional event and used sparingly. (Documentation to support this superior rating is recommended.)

4 - Exceeds Requirements   Performance **consistently meets** job requirements and occasionally exceeds expectations.

3 - Meets Requirements   Performance **meets** job requirements expected of a trained associate and **performs according to expectations**.

2 - Needs Improvement   Performance is **below expectations**. Associate does not consistently meet requirements for work. (A performance improvement plan is required.)

1 - Unsatisfactory   Performance **does not meet requirements** in this area. Associate has performed in a manner **consistently below expectations.** (Documentation should support such an extreme rating. A performance improvement plan is required.)

Section 1: Performance Criteria Ratings

Performance Criteria Job Knowledge   Rating
Extent of understanding job requirements of position and ability to apply knowledge.   _____

_____

_____

_____

_____

Actual Performance/Results

_____

_____

_____

Development

_____

_____

_____

Performance Criteria Productivity/Quality   Rating

Volume of work regularly produced. Promptness and consistency of output, ability to meet deadlines for daily work and _____
projects. Work is accurate, thorough, and neat. Shows good judgment in completing job tasks and following procedures.

_____

_____

_____

_____

Actual Performance/Results

_____

_____

_____

Development

_____

_____

_____

Performance Criteria Dependability/Adaptability   Rating

Conscientious, responsible, and reliable with respect to work completion schedules, as well as attendance. _____
Demonstrates ability to adjust to changing job requirements and/or volume of work.

_____

_____

_____

_____

Actual Performance/Results

_____

_____

_____

Development

_____

_____

_____

Performance Criteria Communication   Rating

Demonstrates ability to interact in a clear and logical manner, verbally and in writing with peers, management, and outside   _____
business contacts.

_____

_____

_____

_____

Actual Performance/Results

_____

_____

_____

Development

_____

_____

_____

Performance Criteria Teamwork and Cooperation   Rating

Establishes constructive relationships with team members. Demonstrates willingness to work with and assist others.   _____
Shows respect for others.

_____

_____

_____

_____

Actual Performance/Results

_____

_____

Development

_____

_____

_____

Performance Criteria Overall Results and Accomplishments   Rating

Describe associate's major accomplishments and cite specific examples of how performance contributed to the department (i.e., examples of excellent/exceptional performance).

_____

_____

_____

_____

Actual Performance/Results

_____

_____

_____

Development

_____

_____

_____

Section 2a: Overall Performance Rating:

Overall Performance Rating: _____ (This should reflect the associate's overall performance.)

Section 2b: Progress toward Goals and Objectives of previous review period:

(Applicable only to associates evaluated last year.)

Describe the progress made by the associate toward previously developed goals and objectives during this period. Indicate the degree of achievement and any factors beyond his/her control that might have contributed to the observed results.

_____

_____

_____

_____

_____

_____

_____

_____

_____

_____

_____

_____

_____

_____

Section 3: Performance and Development Plan for next appraisal period:

A. Development Needs - Describe those aspects of the associate's performance and/or job knowledge in which improvement would contribute to his/her effectiveness and how the associate can improve.

_____

_____

_____

_____

_____

B. List three or more specific goals/objectives that this associate will be expected to accomplish during the next appraisal period (include time-frame action plan, i.e., "Will complete training course by end of first quarter.").

_____

_____

_____

_____

_____

Section 4: Supervisor Comments:

_____

_____

_____

_____

_____

_____

_____

_____

_____

_____

_____

_____

_____

_____

_____

_____

Section 5: Associate Comments:

_____
_____
_____
_____
_____
_____
_____
_____
_____
_____
_____
_____
_____
_____
_____
_____
_____
_____

Associate's Statement: My signature attests to the fact that I have read this evaluation and discussed the content with my supervisor. I have been advised of my performance and of my goals and objectives for the upcoming year.

Associate's Signature: _____   Date: _____

Supervisor's Signature: _____   Date: _____

Employee Name _____

Date _____

Employee Performance Appraisal

Name _____   Department _____

Job Title _____   Date in Position _____

Prepared By _____   Date Given _____

The evaluator's immediate supervisor and Human Resources must review the contents of the appraisal before meeting with the employee.

Next Level Approval _____   Date _____

Human Resources Review _____   Date _____

I met with my supervisor on the date indicated and reviewed this Performance Appraisal in detail. My signature below indicates that the contents were discussed with me but not necessarily my agreement.

Employee Signature _____   Date _____

Evaluator Signature _____   Date _____

Present Rate of Pay: $ _____ Per _____

Merit Increase Percent: _____

New Rate of Pay: $ _____ Per _____

Performance Level Descriptions and Definition

Outstanding   Performance Points: 5   Performance and results achieved **always** exceed the standards and expectations for the position requirements and objectives.

Exceeds Standards   Performance Points: 4   Performance and results achieved **often** exceed the standards and expectations of the position requirements and objectives.

Meets Standards   Performance Points: 3   Performance and results achieved **generally** meet the standards and expectations of the position requirements and objectives.

Below Standards   Performance Points: 2   Performance and results achieved **frequently do not** meet the standards and expectations of the position requirements and objectives.

Unsatisfactory   Performance Points: 1   Performance and results achieved **consistently do not meet** the standards and expectations of the position requirements and objectives.

Weighting Factors

A Weighting Factor: 3   Absolutely essential for success in this job.

B Weighting Factor: 2   Important for success in this job.

C Weighting Factor: 1   Nice to have for success in this job.

Employee Name: _____

Date: _____

Performance Factors

Rate each category separately, including supporting comments
and/or examples demonstrating rating given.

Specific Duties and Responsibilities [From Job Description]	Weight Factor	X	Outstanding	Exceeds Standards	Meets Standards	Below Standards	Un- satisfactory	=	Weighted Score
Job Knowledge and Comprehension: Understands and is knowledgeable of the duties, methods, and procedures required by the job.		X						=	

Comments _____

_____

Work Quality: Completes work assignments thoroughly and completely in an accurate, prompt, neat manner, including standards for verbal/written communications, if applicable.		X						=	

Comments _____

_____

Accuracy: Identifies and corrects errors. Is careful, alert and accurate, paying attention to details of the job.		X						=	

Comments _____

_____

Work Habits: Demonstrates commitment, dedication, cooperation, positive behavior, adaptability, and flexibility with changes in jobs and duties. Considers safety of self and others while working. Takes accountability for job responsibilities.		X						=	

Comments _____

_____

Initiative/Problem Solving/Decision Making: Performs with minimal supervision, acts promptly, seeks solutions to resolve unexpected problems that arise on the job, makes practical, routine decisions.		X						=	

Comments _____

_____

Interpersonal Skills: Demonstrates ability to get along with others, is respectful of co-workers, communicates and acts as a team player, promotes teamwork. Responds and acts appropriately to confrontational situations.		X						=	

Comments _____

_____

	Weight Factor	X	Outstanding	Exceeds Standards	Meets Standards	Below Standards	Un-satisfactory	=	Weighted Score
Attendance and Punctuality: Dependable, arrives at work on time, reports on all scheduled days, adheres to break and meal schedules.*		X						=	
Comments _____									
Time Management: Organizes work well and uses time effectively.		X						=	
Comments _____									
Communication: Openly exchanges information in a timely manner, knows who to keep informed, listens, understands, uses confidential information with discretion, writes and speaks in a clear, concise manner.		X						=	
Comments _____									
Evaluation of Goals/Objectives: Review of business and behavioral goals for this review period and evaluation of results achieved.		X						=	
Comments _____									

Total Points [ ]

*Attendance Record:_____ unscheduled absences, totaling _____ days lost in this review period

Punctuality: _____ times late, including returning late from meals/breaks in this review period

Scheduled Absences: _____ days in this review period

Total Points Earned _____ / **Total Points Possible** _____ = **Score** _____

Hourly employees [evaluated semi-annually]:

Score of 90+%   = 4% raise
Score of 85 – 89.99% = 3.5% raise
Score of 80 – 84.99% = 3% raise
Score of 75 – 79.99% = 2.5% raise
Score of 70 – 74.99% = 2% raise
Score of 65 – 69.99% = 1.5% raise
Score of 60 – 64.99% = 1% raise

Exempt employees, who are evaluated annually, will be eligible for annual raises equal to 2 times the percent above for the equivalent scores.

Scores below 60 will receive no pay increase and will require a Performance Improvement Plan to be reviewed for progress in 30 days.

Special Accomplishments: Describe any accomplishments or special achievements that had significant impact on the department or organization.

_____

_____

_____

_____

_____

Goals and Objectives: State business and behavioral goals and results to be achieved in the coming review period.

_____

_____

_____

_____

_____

Professional Development Review: List any training programs, conferences, or courses attended this year to improve present job skills or for career development.

_____

_____

_____

_____

_____

Identify possible developmental steps for improvement in present job and/or to prepare for future responsibilities.

_____

_____

_____

_____

_____

Employee Comments:

_____

_____

_____

_____

_____

_____

Employee's Signature _____ Date _____

Evaluator's Signature _____ Date _____

Manager's Signature _____ Date _____

Employee Performance Review

Employee's Name: _____   Assessment Date: _____

Evaluation Period, From: _____   To: _____

Employee's Assignment(s) (during evaluation period): _____

Reviewer's Name: _____

Time Interval   ❏ Three or six month review   ❏ Annual review   ❏ Promotion   ❏ Other; Explain:_____

Employee's Signature: _____   Date Signed: _____

Note: Signature verifies the assessment has been discussed with employee.

Corporate Responsibilities

- Follows policies and procedures.
- Completes administrative tasks correctly and on time.
- Supports organization's goals and values.
- Respects diversity/variety.

- Responds to customer's needs, deadlines, and expectations.
- Schedules time off in advance.
- Begins work, meetings, and appointments on time.

Corporate Responsibilities Employee Assessments	Corporate Responsibilities Employer Assessments
❏ Exceeds Expectations ❏ Meets Expectations ❏ Below Expectations	❏ Exceeds Expectations ❏ Meets Expectations ❏ Below Expectations
Comments: _____	Comments:_____

(attach additional pages if necessary)

Communications

- Writes clearly and informatively.
- Edits work for spelling and grammar.
- Varies writing style to meet requirements.

- Demonstrates group presentation skills.
- Participates in meetings.
- Speaks clearly, listens to details, and gets clarification.

Communications Employee Assessments	Communications Employer Assessments
❏ Exceeds Expectations ❏ Meets Expectations ❏ Below Expectations	❏ Exceeds Expectations ❏ Meets Expectations ❏ Below Expectations
Comments: _____	Comments:_____

(attach additional pages if necessary)

Planning and Organization

- Works in an organized manner, uses time effectively.
- Develops project plans and personal task activities.
- Meets commitments and responds to customers' needs.
- Integrates changes smoothly.
- Shows initiative and a positive "can-do" attitude.

Planning and Organization Employee Assessments	Planning and Organization Employer Assessments
❑ Exceeds Expectations ❑ Meets Expectations ❑ Below Expectations	❑ Exceeds Expectations ❑ Meets Expectations ❑ Below Expectations
Comments: _____	Comments: _____

(attach additional pages if necessary)

Technical Knowledge

- Competent in required job skills and knowledge.
- Exhibits ability to learn and apply new skills.
- Shares technical knowledge with others.
- Understands customers' business domain.
- Understands company's resources and capabilities.
- Stays apprised of new and current developments.
- Uses technology to improve effectiveness/productivity.

Technical Knowledge Employee Assessments	Technical Knowledge Employer Assessments
❑ Exceeds Expectations ❑ Meets Expectations ❑ Below Expectations	❑ Exceeds Expectations ❑ Meets Expectations ❑ Below Expectations
Comments: _____	Comments: _____

(attach additional pages if necessary)

Leadership

- Exhibits confidence in self and others.
- Inspires respect and trust.
- Motivates others to perform well.

- Reacts well under pressure.
- Has initiative to take action.

Leadership Employee Assessments

☐ Exceeds Expectations   ☐ Meets Expectations   ☐ Below Expectations

Comments: _____

_____

_____

_____

_____

Leadership Employer Assessments

☐ Exceeds Expectations   ☐ Meets Expectations   ☐ Below Expectations

Comments: _____

_____

_____

_____

_____

(attach additional pages if necessary)

Teamwork

- Establishes and maintains effective relations.
- Exhibits tact and consideration.
- Displays positive outlook and pleasant manner.
- Offers support to co-workers and customers.
- Works actively to resolve conflicts.

- Volunteers readily and seeks increased responsibilities.
- Looks for and takes advantage of opportunities.
- Will seek and ask for help when needed.
- Generates suggestions and innovative ideas.

Teamwork Employee Assessments

☐ Exceeds Expectations   ☐ Meets Expectations   ☐ Below Expectations

Comments: _____

_____

_____

_____

_____

Teamwork Employer Assessments

☐ Exceeds Expectations   ☐ Meets Expectations   ☐ Below Expectations

Comments: _____

_____

_____

_____

_____

(attach additional pages if necessary)

Overall Expectations

Overall Employee Assessments

☐ Exceeds Expectations   ☐ Meets Expectations   ☐ Below Expectations

Comments: _____

_____

_____

_____

_____

Overall Employer Assessments

☐ Exceeds Expectations   ☐ Meets Expectations   ☐ Below Expectations

Comments: _____

_____

_____

_____

_____

(attach additional pages if necessary)

Additional Assessments or Comments

Additional Assessments or Comments

Additional Assessments or Comments Employee Assessments	Additional Assessments or Comments Employer Assessments
Comments: _____	Comments:_____
_____	_____
_____	_____
_____	_____
_____	_____

(attach additional pages if necessary)

1. Recommendations for professional/career development (training, seminars, etc.): _____

_____

_____

_____

_____

_____

2. Professional goals and objectives (short-term 6–12 months – be specific): _____

_____

_____

_____

_____

_____

3. Describe your current job responsibilities (attach additional pages if necessary): _____

_____

_____

_____

_____

_____

Performance Appraisal – Non-Exempt

Employee: _____   Date of Hire: _____

Department: _____   Job Title: _____

Supervisor: _____

Review Period: From _____   To _____

Purpose: The purpose of conducting the Performance Appraisal is to 1) Develop better communication between the employee and the supervisor; 2) Improve the quality of work; 3) Increase productivity; and 4) Promote employee development.

Performance Rating Categories: Consider the employee's performance in each category and designate the level of performance that most accurately describes his/her job performance. Give careful consideration to each category before choosing the rating. The following is a description of each level of performance:

- **Outstanding**—consistently exceeds job expectations
- **Commendable**—exceeds minimal requirements of the job
- **Meets requirements**—proficient in the job function

- **Needs improvement**—fails to perform the job at an acceptable level
- **Unsatisfactory job performance**—consistently fails to perform the job at an acceptable level; does not meet minimal requirements

Productivity and Cost Effectiveness:

	Outstanding	Commendable	Meets Requirements	Needs Improvement	Unsatisfactory
	❏	❏	❏	❏	❏

Amount of acceptable work performed; minimizes or eliminates waste? performs as efficiently as possible without jeopardizing quality; volume as directed? more than expected? less than expected? recommends areas where productivity can be improved?

Comments: _____

_____

_____

_____

_____

Job Knowledge:

	Outstanding	Commendable	Meets Requirements	Needs Improvement	Unsatisfactory
	❏	❏	❏	❏	❏

Skills and knowledge required for the job; ability to understand the required duties, responsibilities, skills, and procedures.

Comments: _____

_____

_____

_____

_____

Quality of Work:

	Outstanding	Commendable	Meets Requirements	Needs Improvement	Unsatisfactory
	❏	❏	❏	❏	❏

Thoroughness and accuracy of work performed; performed to established standards? Work needs redoing? Mistakes made?

Comments: _____

_____

_____

_____

_____

Teamwork:

	Outstanding	Commendable	Meets Requirements	Needs Improvement	Unsatisfactory
	❏	❏	❏	❏	❏

Cooperation and flexibility; works helpfully with others? responds positively to supervision? actively contributes to team's goals? offers/accepts constructive criticism? makes effort to comply with direction?

Comments: _____

_____

_____

_____

_____

Dependability and Attendance:

	Outstanding	Commendable	Meets Requirements	Needs Improvement	Unsatisfactory
	❏	❏	❏	❏	❏

Consistency in carrying out assignments; punctuality and no unexcused absences? follows through on assignments? delivers full day's work as assigned? adheres to work rules?

Comments: _____

_____

_____

_____

_____

Initiative:

	Outstanding	Commendable	Meets Requirements	Needs Improvement	Unsatisfactory
	❏	❏	❏	❏	❏

Interest and willingness to learn; does what needs to be done without being asked? takes responsibility for independent action? anticipates potential problems/opportunities? requires little/infrequent supervision to be productive? seeks additional assignments when other tasks are completed?

Comments: _____

_____

_____

_____

_____

Safety and Cleanliness of Work Area:

	Outstanding	Commendable	Meets Requirements	Needs Improvement	Unsatisfactory
	❏	❏	❏	❏	❏

Wears proper PPE; works in a safe manner by adhering to safety guidelines; operates equipment and machines in a safe manner; maintains a clean work area; organizes work area at the end of each work day without being asked?

Comments: _____

_____

_____

_____

_____

Overall Performance:

Outstanding	Commendable	Meets Requirements	Needs Improvement	Unsatisfactory
❏	❏	❏	❏	❏

Comment on the overall results and areas for development.
Suggest actions that will help.

Comments: _____

_____

_____

_____

_____

Employee Comments:

_____

_____

_____

_____

_____

_____

_____

_____

_____

_____

_____

_____

_____

_____

_____

_____

_____

_____

_____

_____

_____

Employee Signature:_____ Date: _____

(Your signature indicates that the appraisal was reviewed and discussed with you.)

Supervisor Signature: _____ Date: _____

Manager Signature: _____ Date: _____

HR: _____

Employee Performance Appraisal

Employee Name:_____   **Position/Department:** _____

Date of Hire: _____   **Date Completing Review:** _____

Ratings: Please rate the employee on the factors listed below, using the following rating codes:

1   = Unsatisfactory/Fails to meet minimum requirements
2   = Acceptable, but needs improvement to meet requirements
3   = Meets expected requirements
4   = Generally exceeds requirements
5   = Far exceeds requirements
N/A = Not Applicable or too soon to rate employee on criteria

1 2 3 4 5 N/A   **1. Adaptability** (Adjusts to changing situations, learns new and different tasks)

1 2 3 4 5 N/A   **2. Attitude** (Shows enthusiasm toward the job; works overtime when asked by supervisor)

1 2 3 4 5 N/A   **3. Communication** (Speaks and writes in a clear and concise manner as it pertains to the job)

1 2 3 4 5 N/A   **4. Attendance** (Does not disrupt operations by being habitually tardy or absent; works as scheduled)

1 2 3 4 5 N/A   **5. Conduct** (Follows company's rules and policies and is a good example for co-workers to follow)

1 2 3 4 5 N/A   **6. Initiative/Judgment** (Identifies and appropriately solves or refers problems)

1 2 3 4 5 N/A   **7. Interpersonal Skills** (Works effectively with other employees in a harmonious manner)

1 2 3 4 5 N/A   **8. Job Knowledge** (Understands and performs all elements of the job)

1 2 3 4 5 N/A   **9. Work Quality** (Accuracy and reliability of results)

1 2 3 4 5 N/A   **10. Work Quantity** (Meets or exceeds production standards; completes work in a timely manner)

1 2 3 4 5 N/A   **11. Safety** (Promotes and reinforces a safe work environment; displays good housekeeping in work area)

_____   **Total Points**

Overall Performance Rating:

❏ **Unsatisfactory** (0–15 pts)
Does not meet the key requirements of the job. Excessive direction and follow-up are needed.
Immediate improvement required.   **No Increase Awarded at This Time**

❏ **Needs Improvement** (16–31 pts)
Met the key requirements, but did not meet job requirements in all areas. Performance is   **Increase: 1.5–2.5%**
inconsistent and at times fails to meet the standards of the job.

❏ **Meets Requirements** (32–37 pts)
Met the job requirements in all key areas. Performance consistently meets the standards of the job.   **Increase: 2.5–4.0%**

❏ **Exceeds Requirements** (38–48 pts)
Met the key requirements of the job in all areas and exceeded the requirements of the job in   **Increase: 3.5–5.0%**
many areas. Performance is characterized by consistent high achievement.

❏ **Far Exceeds Requirements** (49–55 pts)
Far exceeded the requirements in all areas. Performance consistently by exceptional accomplishment.   **Increase: 4.5–6.0%**

Note: Increase % noted above are to be used as a guideline only. Increases are at the discretion of the supervisor; any major increase percentages that are not close to above guidelines must be pre-approved by the department head or HR before given to employee.

Major Strengths:

Describe the employee's major strengths and abilities and how they relate to the job requirements. _____

_____

_____

_____

_____

Areas Requiring Improvement:

Describe the specific areas in which you feel the employee needs to improve. Also describe the specific actions that will be taken by you and the employee to strengthen these areas, any training required, and the deadline for which improvements are expected.

_____

_____

_____

_____

Goals:

List the goals to be accomplished during the up-coming year.

_____

_____

_____

_____

Employee Comments: *(Optional)*

_____

_____

_____

_____

Required Signatures:

Employee: _____   **Date:** _____

Reviewer: _____   **Date:** _____

Approval/Witness: _____   **Date:** _____
(If required)

E. Job Duty or Goal-Based Reviews

The forms in this section ask the supervisor to define the performance factors for the review. This approach can take the supervisor longer to complete, especially the first time it is done for an employee. The advantage is that the review is specifically related to the job the employee is performing.

1. **Performance Evaluation Form:** Provides space for up to five job-specific performance factors, page 97

2. **Yearly Performance Review:** Lists individual goals and asks both the supervisor and the employee to comment on progress toward them, page 99

3. **Employee Performance Appraisal Program:** Provides three performance categories of primary job responsibilities, performance based on global values, and performance based on goals and projects, plus space for a professional growth and development plan, page 101

4. **Performance Review:** Starts with a description of the employee's job and provides space for discussion about progress toward expected results, page 109

5. **Essay Evaluation Employee Performance Discussion:** Lists essential job functions and provides space for supervisor to discuss accomplishments, strengths, opportunities for improvement, and input from colleagues, page 113

6. **Review of Accomplishments:** Focuses on key objectives, page 119

7. **Performance Review:** Emphasizes feedback on overall progress toward total job outcome and involves employee and manager feedback, page 129

8. **Performance Review Guidelines:** Divides feedback into two major categories, page 133

Performance Evaluation Form

Name_____ Job Title _____

Manager _____ Department _____

Review Period: From _____ To _____

Purpose of Review   ❑ Introductory   ❑ Annual Performance   ❑ Other _____

Score the performance in each job factor below on a scale of 5 – 1, as follows:

5 = Outstanding, consistently exceeds this job factor expectations and is recognized by peers and/or customers as a leader and positive example for others.

4 = Above Expectations, consistently meets and occasionally exceeds this job factor expectations.

3 = Meets Expectations, consistently meets this job factor expectations.

2 = Below Expectations, occasionally fails to meet this job factor expectations.

1 = Needs Improvement, consistently fails to meet this job factor expectations and a job performance improvement plan is required.

Section 1 – Job Performance (60% of total score)   Score   Points

Enter up to five job knowledge and skill factors from the job description

- _____   _____

- _____   _____

- _____   _____

- _____   _____

- _____   _____

- Quality of Work   _____

- Quantity of Work   _____

- Negotiable Item   _____

                                       Average Score =   _____ **x 12 =** _____

Comments: _____

_____

_____

Section 2 – Personal Performance (20% of total score)   Score   Points

- Dependability   _____

- Attendance and Punctuality   _____

- Interpersonal Skills   _____

- Flexibility   _____

- Communication Skills   _____

- Teamwork   _____

- Customer Service   _____

- Negotiable Item   _____

                                       Average Score =   _____ **x 4 =** _____

Comments: _____

_____

_____

Section 3 – Personal Improvement (20% of total score)   Score   Points

- Support of a "Change" Environment   _____ •
- Support of Continuous Quality Improvement   _____ •
- Professional Growth   _____ •
- Developmental Goals Accomplishment   _____ •
- Negotiable Item   _____ •

                                                  Average Score = _____ **x 4 =** _____

Comments: _____

_____

_____

Points from **section 1** _____ + **section 2** _____ + **section 3** _____ = _____ **Total**

Developmental Goals for next review period

1. _____

2. _____

3. _____

Signatures

Employee _____ **Date** _____

Employee Comments _____

_____

_____

_____

_____

_____

_____

_____

_____

_____

Supervisor/Manager _____ **Date** _____

Next Level Head _____ **Date** _____

Human Resources _____ **Date** _____

Yearly Performance Review

Employee's Name: _____ Title: _____ Date: _____

[Company Slogan] means performing our jobs to the best of our abilities. Periodic discussions with our supervisors are important so that we can evaluate how we are doing. This form is intended to guide your self-evaluation, your supervisor's evaluation of your work, and lead the two of you through a meaningful performance and development discussion each year.

Learning:

- Assumes responsibility for own learning.
- Learns quickly with demonstrated thorough understanding of concepts.
- Integrates and applies new and existing knowledge, skills, and abilities.

Comment: _____

_____

_____

Quality:

- Demonstrates proficiency in all phases of this job and related jobs.
- Demonstrates a high degree of accuracy and thoroughness in work.
- Continually strives to improve work product quality to meet changing customer needs.

Comment: _____

_____

_____

Productivity:

- Demonstrates a high degree of productivity.
- Meets deadlines and assumes personal responsibility for work product.
- Continually strives to improve efficiency.

Comment: _____

_____

_____

Dependability:

- Maintains consistent work attendance.
- Demonstrates reliability under normal and ever-changing job circumstances.
- Consistently offers to assist peers and other work groups when needed.

Comment: _____

_____

_____

Cooperation:

- Consistently operates outside of own self-interests.
- Maintains cooperative working relationships with peers, management, and customers.
- Demonstrates flexibility and consideration during interactions with peers, management, and customers.

Comment: _____

_____

_____

[Company Goals]

In what area(s) does the employee perform especially well?

_____

_____

_____

In what areas should the employee focus his/her development (talents and/or weaknesses)?

_____

_____

_____

What added training or experience is needed to enhance the employee's performance?

_____

_____

_____

Standards of Performance — Optional

Instructions: _In some instances, it may be appropriate for the employee to set his/her own standards, which should be approved by the supervisor. Standards are key goals, which the employee will concentrate on to support company objectives. The standards are not meant to be all-inclusive of the job description. There will be multiple areas of the job not included in these standards, which may be just as important as the standards detailed here. Standards should be **brief, simple** (straightforward, uncomplicated), **specific** (avoid generalizations), **quantifiable** (should be measurable), **timed** (set deadlines), and **few** (three is optimal)._

Individual Goals _Rank order if warranted_

_____

_____

_____

_____

_____

Additional Comments

Supervisor's Comments

_____

_____

_____

Supervisor's Signature	Date

Employee's Comments

_____

_____

_____

Employee's Signature	Date

Employee Performance Appraisal Program
Confidential

Employee: _____

Job Title: _____

Evaluator: _____ Date: _____

Employee Performance Appraisal Process

Introduction

[Company's] performance appraisal process has three fundamental objectives:

- To assess and measure individual performance on the job

- To identify opportunities for improvement and advancement

- To develop professional skills through open and constructive feedback

Optimal job performance requires a clear understanding of what work is to be performed, desired outcomes, and how well the work is completed (e.g., quality of the work, level of production, contribution to the organization, adherence to corporate values, etc.). The performance appraisal process ensures that employee and team leader/manager expectations are aligned. Through this process, the employee and team leader/manager can find opportunities to work together to improve job performance and grow professionally within the organization.

The appraisal process includes four components:

I. **Job Responsibilities** focus on measuring performance related to current job accountabilities, duties. This section asks for an evaluation of each major area of responsibility from a formal job description.

II. **Values Behaviors** focuses on the behaviors that typify [Company's] core values. Generally, strengths (and weaknesses) in behavioral areas are consistent with strong (and weak) job performance. However, an individual may achieve significant results while still demonstrating negative behaviors inconsistent with our values and culture.

III. **Goals and Projects** is an optional section used to evaluate performance against specific goals and projects assigned during a particular year. Such goals/projects are regularly present in management level positions. However, we encourage all employees to consider participating in at least one goal or project outside of normal work duties.

IV. **Professional Development and Growth Plan** asks you to establish developmental areas of growth or educational goals for the upcoming year. You and your team leader/manager must discuss and agree on this plan.

On the final page of this document, the team leader/manager enters an overall performance rating, based on the information completed in the preceding sections. Each team leader/manager must discuss ratings in each section of the appraisal, as well as the final rating, with employees. Then the appropriate General Manager reviews the performance appraisals. Finally, a Human Resource representative files a copy of the performance appraisal in the employee's personnel file. Note: nothing in this appraisal process alters the "at-will" employment relationship.

I.   Performance of Primary Job Responsibilities

This section is designed to evaluate how well an individual performs the responsibilities required of the position. It focuses on duties and accountabilities and their relative importance. Using the scale below, assess the individual's performance for each duty. The rating should then be multiplied by the "Relative Importance" or Weighted Average (%). A total score is calculated by adding values in the "Calculation" column.

Rating Scale

4 = Exceeds expectations: Results and behaviors are exceptional and particularly valuable to the organization; this person is a role model. Performance is routinely ahead of schedule, innovative, cost-conscious, and participative.

3 = Fully competent: Meets and periodically exceeds expectations. This person is a strong contributor, and is eager, helpful, prompt, and conscientious.

2 = Meets most requirements: Some areas require attention and improvement. Performance at this level provides an acceptable contribution. Work is usually on time, and of adequate quality; behavior is willing.

1 = Needs improvement: Performance of this duty or behavior does not meet reasonable expectations and company standards. Employees must take immediate steps to improve. Failure to do so may result in formal corrective actions.

Primary Responsibilities and Accountabilities	%Wt.	Observations/ Improvement Plan	Rating	Calculation

Total Rating for This Section: _____

II. Evaluation of Performance Based on [Company] Values

[Company's] vision is [Company Vision Statement]. One important way this is accomplished is by adhering to [Company's] core values. Global values motivate and guide actions. They define how [Company] employees choose to treat each other, customers, and vendors in accomplishing goals. While the previous section evaluated *what* individuals accomplish, this section defines *how* individuals perform their jobs. The following job behaviors reflect the various components of [Company's] values. Using the rating scale below, assign a score for each job behavior listed.

Rating Scale

4 = Exceeds expectations: Results and behaviors are exceptional and particularly valuable to the organization; this person is a role model. Performance is routinely ahead of schedule, innovative, cost-conscious, and participative.

3 = Fully competent: Meets and periodically exceeds expectations. This person is a strong contributor and is eager, helpful, prompt, and conscientious.

2 = Meets most requirements: Some areas of performance warrant attention and improvement. Performance at this level provides an acceptable contribution. Work is usually on time, and of adequate quality; behavior is polite.

1 = Needs improvement: Performance of this duty or behavior does not meet reasonable expectations and company standards. Employees must take immediate steps to improve. Failure to do so may result in formal corrective actions.

[Company] Values

Integrity – Teamwork – Communication – Equal Opportunity – Accountability, Pride, and Ownership – Exceed Customer Expectations

Evaluator Rating	Job Behavior
	Integrity – Demonstrating respect and trust of others. Example behaviors include: • Being honest about your mistakes, your strengths and limitations. • Demonstrating trust in others. **Comments/Other Examples** _____ _____ _____ _____
	Teamwork – Cooperation and Positive Attitude. Example behaviors include: • Willingly participates in group work activities. • Seeks to collaborate and offers assistance to others on a regular basis. • Always willing to keep trying. **Comments/Other Examples** _____ _____ _____ _____
	Communication – Open, honest feedback. Example behaviors include: • Freely shares ideas and information. • Is approachable, listens and considers the ideas of others. • Listens to criticism and directions; reacts appropriately. **Comments/Other Examples** _____ _____ _____ _____

Evaluator Rating	Job Behavior
	Equal Opportunity – Advancement, Employment, and Involvement. Example behaviors include: • Regularly looks for ways to involve others. • Proactive in pursuing own professional growth. **Comments/Other Examples** _____ _____ _____ _____
	Exceeds Customer Expectations – Example behaviors include: • Passionate about resolving customer's problems. **Comments/Other Examples** _____ _____ _____ _____
	Accountability, Pride, and Ownership – Competent Leadership at All Levels; Knowledgeable Employees; Acknowledges Work Performance; Responsible Community Involvement. Example behaviors include: • Seeks out training and new information to improve self and work. • Keeps work and area neat and clean. • Proactively solves work problems. **Comments/Other Examples** _____ _____ _____ _____

Total Rating for This Section: _____

III. Performance on Goals and Projects

This section is used to evaluate goals, special assignments, or committee involvement performed during a particular year. Many goals or special assignments are regularly present in management level positions. However, we encourage all employees to consider having at least one goal or project to work on during the upcoming year.

In the space provided below, briefly summarize each goal or special assignment that demands significant time and effort during the evaluation period. Then, using the rating scale below, apply the score that best describes the degree of success on each item. If the assignment was not completed during the evaluation period, evaluate progress to date.

Rating Scale

4 = Exceeds expectations: Results and behaviors are exceptional and particularly valuable to the organization; this person is a role model. Performance is routinely ahead of schedule, innovative, cost-conscious, and participative.

3 = Fully competent: Meets and periodically exceeds expectations. This person is a strong contributor, and is eager, helpful, prompt, and conscientious.

2 = Meets most requirements: Some areas require attention and improvement. Performance at this level provides an acceptable contribution. Work is usually on time, and of adequate quality; behavior is willing.

1 = Needs improvement: Performance of this duty or behavior does not meet reasonable expectations and company standards. Employees must take immediate steps to improve. Failure to do so may result in formal corrective actions.

Goal or Project	%Wt.	Observations	Rating	Calculation

Total Rating for This Section: _____

IV. Professional Development and Growth Plan

This section will establish a professional growth plan for the individual. Using the space provided, list and briefly describe performance objectives for the upcoming year. Next to these objectives, list any areas of performance, including those associated with goals or special assignments, that the employee and the team leader/manager agree need to be further developed. Also include aspects of values behavior that could be enhanced. This section should also include career growth considerations in the form of listing special projects, other potential job positions, or promotional opportunities. Associated with this list, mention any classes, seminars, or other ways that this employee could work toward developing skills. Achieving these objectives should enhance the individual's knowledge, skills, experience, and professional capability in a way that improves job performance, now and in the future.

Performance Objectives	Performance Improvement Areas	Career Opportunities	Specific Development Strategies

Final Performance Rating

The relative importance of Sections I and III must be calculated in advance of the appraisal and agreed to by the employee and the Team Leader/Manager. The total relative importance must equal 100%. The combined percentage for Sections I and III cannot exceed 80%, and the relative importance of Section II (value-based job behaviors) must be 20%.

Insert the weighted ratings from Sections I and III and the Average Rating from Section II into the Chart below. Then multiply each rating by its relative importance. Write the result in the Calculation column. Add the values in the Calculation column to determine the Final Employee Performance Rating.

	Relative Importance	Rating	Calculation
Weighted Average Rating from Section I			
Average Rating from Section II			
Weighted Average Rating from Section III			
Total:			
Final Employee Performance Rating:			

Signatures and Approvals

Employee _____ Date _____

This signature acknowledges that I participated in a review meeting.

Additional Comments: _____

_____

_____

_____

_____

_____

Employee Comments: _____

_____

_____

_____

_____

_____

Group Leader/Team Leader/Manager_____ Date _____

General Manager _____ Date _____

Note: If the Rater is a GM, the performance appraisal must be reviewed by the sponsoring Managing Director.

Performance Review

Employee Name:_____

Position: _____

❑ Exempt   ❑ Non-exempt (To be indicated by the human resources department.)

Date of Hire: _____

Date of Review: _____

Manager: _____

Performance Review Form

The purpose of the Employee Performance Review is to foster and improve performance of employees by providing opportunities for communication and goal setting and by clearly defining the performance requirements of the position. Additionally, performance reviews provide a periodic, written record of employee performance, to make them aware of supervisory appraisals of their work.

This is a narrative format where supervisors provide written feedback and comments in an open-ended fashion. Each section should be completed and specific examples should be used whenever possible.

The overall job performance should be documented, including highlights of performance during the rating period, outstanding achievements, areas needing improvement, and other related information considered noteworthy. There is a section provided for employee comments/feedback as well.

A. This section is provided to document the job description of the position.

Job Description *(include primary duty – summary/purpose, essential job function; responsibilities and accountabilities; level of independence, discretion and judgment; any direct reports, how many?; specific skills required) keep it brief…*

_____

_____

_____

_____

_____

_____

_____

_____

B. This section is provided to document quantifiable results accomplished by the employee.

Results Expected   **Results Achieved (Include key accomplishments here)**

_____   _____

_____   _____

_____   _____

_____   _____

_____   _____

_____   _____

C. Use this section to describe any development activity that occurred during the performance period to improve performance in the employee's current position or to prepare him/her for future assignments.

Development Recap

_____

_____

_____

_____

D. This section is provided to document developmental needs related to job-specific skills or attributes and goals for the next period.

Examples: technical skills, innovative thinking skills, interpersonal skills, oral and written communication skills, initiative, business acumen, listening skills, analytical skills, decision making skills, administrative skills, flexibility, team player, customer service skills, problem solving skills.

Areas of Development   **Goals for the Next Period**

_____   _____

_____   _____

_____   _____

_____   _____

_____   _____

E. This section is used as the overall summary of the employee's performance in his/her current role.

1 Consistently Below Expectations
2 Below Expectations
3 Meets Expectations
4 Exceeds Expectations
5 Far Exceeds Expectations

Reliability	Quality of Work	Planning	Self Management	Creativity	Determination	Teamwork	Productivity	Job Knowledge	Overall Score (average)

(whole number)

Performance Descriptions

Consistently Below Expectations	Below Expectations	Meets Expectations	Exceeds Expectations	Far Exceeds Expectations
Performance is unacceptable.	Achieved some objectives, but missed significant others.	Achieved objectives.	Achieved all objectives and exceeded some.	Significantly exceeded objectives.
Requirements of the position have not been met.	Demonstrated some requisite skills, knowledge, and experience, but lacks significant others.	Demonstrated requisite skills and knowledge and applied them to achieve objectives.	Demonstrated all requisite skills and knowledge and took initiative to enhance or increase skills.	Applied highly developed skills and extensive knowledge to achieve objectives.
Performance improvement plan is necessary.	Willingness to develop requisite skills, knowledge, or experience is in question. Individual still learning the job.	Achievement of objectives required more coaching than normally expected.	Sought out innovative solutions to accomplish objectives. Incorporated continuous improvement into results.	Continually enhanced skills. Produced extraordinary results. Served as role model and mentor through active knowledge transfer. Helped others develop skills.

F.   This section is provided to give employees the opportunity to add any comments or feedback regarding the performance review.

Employee Comments _____

_____

_____

_____

_____

_____

Manager's Signature   Date

_____

Employee's Signature   Date

Performance Planning

Employee Name: _____   **Performance Period:** [Quarterly] _____

Goals	Measures	Results Achieved

Essay Evaluation Employee Performance Discussion—Instructions

Essay Evaluation
An essay evaluation is a self-evaluation of an employee's performance by the employee, with optional input from subordinates, peers, and customers (internal/external). The optional input comprises 360-Degree feedback. Each employee is responsible for initiating the process, scheduling a meeting with his/her manager to discuss the evaluation, and ensuring that the completed evaluation reaches the Human Resources Department. The following outlines some guidelines for completing this process:

Informational Section
Completed by Human Resources. If you have any questions, please contact [HR Employee Name].

Section I
Start by listing the essential functions and/or goals of your job. Use your Position Content Summary (PCS) as a reference, if available. If there are more than 5, create additional space in the document.

Section II
Next, cite some of your most successful accomplishments during the performance discussion period.

Note: Before proceeding any further, schedule a short meeting with your manager to discuss the essential functions/goals and most successful accomplishments. It is important that the two of you reach a consensus of opinion on these items before proceeding.

Section III
Discuss some of your strengths and how you can further utilize those strengths in the coming year.

Section IV
Identify areas where you could have handled things better, more efficiently, more timely, etc.

Section V
Optional. Obtain feedback from peers, subordinates, internal or external customers. You can either obtain the comments verbally and record them on your form, send a blank electronic copy and have them complete it electronically, returning comments to your manager or yourself, and then copy their comments into your master form.

Section VI
Write down your goals and/or expectations for the coming year.

Section VII
Write down your thoughts on short-term (12–18 months) training and learning opportunities.

Section VIII
Write down your thoughts on longer-term (2–3 years) career development desires. What's the next job or role you'd like to pursue? Where do you want your career to go?

Next Steps
Contact your direct manager to schedule time to meet to discuss your evaluation. Be sure to send your self-evaluation to your supervisor ahead of time so that he/she can be prepared to discuss the evaluation. During this meeting, you and your manager should reach consensus on the points covered in the evaluation.

Section IX
This area is for signatures of the employee, direct manager, and indirect manager.

Section X

This area is for the direct manager to make comments.

Section XI

This area is for the employee to make comments.

Section XII

This area is for the indirect manager to make comments.

Next Steps

Employee and manager should sign performance discussion at time of performance discussion meeting. Employee and manager have five days to comment and send the completed form to the Indirect Manager for signature and comments. Copies of the performance discussion can be copied with the original copy sent to [Employee Name] in HR by [Date].

If you have any questions concerning this process, please contact [HR Employee Name].

Essay Evaluation Employee Performance Discussion—Form

Name: _____   Department: _____

Job Title: _____

Salary Plan: _____   Job Level: _____

Performance Discussion Period: _____   Performance Discussion Date: _____

Manager's Name: _____   Job Title: _____

I. List the most essential job functions or goals for the past year:

    1.) _____

    2.) _____

    3.) _____

    4.) _____

    5.) _____

II. Cite examples of the most successful job accomplishments since last review:

    1.) _____

    2.) _____

    3.) _____

    4.) _____

    5.) _____

III. Discuss strengths and how to further leverage those strengths:

_____

_____

_____

_____

_____

_____

_____

_____

IV. Discuss opportunities for improvement:

_____

_____

_____

_____

_____

_____

_____

_____

V. 360-Degree Comments: *(Optional)*

1.) _____
_____
_____

2.) _____
_____
_____

3.) _____
_____
_____

4.) _____
_____
_____

5.) _____
_____
_____

VI. Employee Performance Plan: Goals and expectations for coming year.

_____
_____
_____
_____
_____
_____
_____
_____

VII. Employee Development Plan: Short-term (12–18 months) training and learning opportunities.

_____
_____
_____
_____
_____
_____
_____
_____

VIII. Employee Development Plan: (longer-term (2–3 years) career development; potential future job roles, experiences, opportunities)

_____

_____

_____

_____

_____

_____

_____

IX: Employee Evaluation (Signatures):

Employee: _____ Date: _____
(Employee's signature indicates that performance discussion took place.)

Manager: _____ Date: _____

Indirect Manager: _____ Date: _____

X. Comments from Direct Manager:

_____

_____

_____

_____

_____

_____

_____

_____

_____

_____

XI. Comments from Employee:

_____

_____

_____

_____

_____

_____

_____

_____

_____

_____

XII. Comments from Indirect Manager:

_____

_____

_____

_____

_____

_____

_____

_____

_____

_____

_____

_____

Review of Accomplishments—Instructions

The attached performance review template is designed to streamline [Company's] performance appraisal process. Managers may modify the template as needed. However, all performance review forms must include the following elements: employee information, review of retrospective objectives, an overall rating, appropriate signatures, an area for employee comments, and prospective objectives.

Template Instructions:

The template includes the following sections:

- **Review of Accomplishments** [page number]. Use this section to review past objectives. List the objective in the space provided and answer the questions associated with each objective. Consider the skills and capabilities used to meet the objectives. A list of skills and capabilities is included on [page number]. Your answers should be short and specific; two or three sentences is fine. Use examples that best illustrate the performance on each objective.

- **Objective Setting** [page number]. This is where you document future objectives. Managers and employees should work together to write the go-forward objectives. Make sure the objectives are specific and measurable, and are aligned with the department's objectives. Include milestones and a target completion date. Review objectives frequently. Employees should notify their manager when the objectives need to be updated or changed. Don't wait until next year's review to update the objectives.

- **Discussion Tools** [page number]. The discussion tools will help both employees and managers prepare for the performance appraisal meeting. Review the list of appraisal topics on [page number] and the skills and capabilities on [page number] through [page number] as you plan the appraisal meeting.

- **Process Flow Chart.** A flow chart of the recommended performance appraisal process is included on the last page.

Manager Instructions:

This process is designed to encourage employee involvement. Employees should participate in the process and provide feedback concerning their performance. Employees may complete all or part of the template and forward it to you prior to the their formal performance review. Managers are responsible for all content included in the final documentation. Managers are also responsible for ensuring that the review is completed on time.

Review of Accomplishments—Form

Employee Name _____

Department _____

Job Title _____ Length of Time in Position _____

Today's Date _____ Review Date _____ Date of Last Review_____

❏ Annual Review   ❏ Other (please explain) _____

List each key objective or major job responsibility with a few words and a couple of specific examples after each question. This is intended for use by employee and manager to discuss the major elements of job performance.

Key Objective/Responsibility (please summarize): _____

_____

_____

_____

Was the objective met? _____

Please list 2–3 examples of what went well: _____

_____

_____

_____

What do you think could have gone better? _____

_____

What skills and capabilities were used effectively? (See [page number] for examples) _____

_____

What skills and capabilities can be developed to increase effectiveness? _____

_____

Comments: _____

_____

_____

_____

Key Objective/Responsibility (please summarize): _____

_____

_____

_____

Was the objective met? _____

Please list 2–3 examples of what went well: _____

_____

_____

_____

What do you think could have gone better? _____

_____

What skills and capabilities were used effectively? (See [page number] for examples) _____

_____

What skills and capabilities can be developed to increase effectiveness? _____

_____

Comments: _____

_____

_____

_____

Key Objective/Responsibility (please summarize): _____

_____

_____

_____

Was the objective met? _____

Please list 2–3 examples of what went well: _____

_____

_____

_____

What do you think could have gone better? _____

_____

What skills and capabilities were used effectively? _____

_____

What skills and capabilities can be developed to increase effectiveness? (See [page number] for examples) _____

_____

Comments: _____

_____

_____

_____

Key Objective/Responsibility (please summarize): _____

_____

_____

_____

Was the objective met? _____

Please list 2–3 examples of what went well: _____

_____

_____

_____

What do you think could have gone better? _____

_____

What skills and capabilities were used effectively? (See [page number] for examples) _____

_____

What skills and capabilities can be developed to increase effectiveness? _____

_____

Comments: _____

_____

_____

_____

Employee Comments: _____

_____

_____

_____

_____

_____

_____

_____

_____

_____

_____

_____

_____

_____

_____

Check the box that best summarizes this employee's level of accomplishment relating to stated objectives and relevant skills and abilities.

❏   Performance improvement required - 1

❏   Focused development necessary - 2

❏   Meets expectations and objectives appropriately - 3

❏   Highly effective performer - 4

❏   Exceeds expectations consistently - 5

Appraiser Signature _____ Date_____

Account Manager Initials _____ Date_____

Second-Level Manager Signature _____ Date_____

Employee Signature _____ Date_____

Objective Setting

Employee Name _____ Date_____

Manager Name _____ Date for Follow-Up _____

List each major job responsibility. For each objective/responsibility, negotiate and specify results to be achieved, and include a date for completion if applicable. Remember to make each objective specific, measurable, and action-oriented. This information will be the basis for on-going performance communication.

Key Objective/Responsibility #1:

- _____
- _____
- _____

Target date: _____

Key Objective/Responsibility #2:

- _____
- _____
- _____

Target date: _____

Key Objective/Responsibility #3:

- _____
- _____
- _____

Target date: _____

Key Objective/Responsibility #4:

- _____
- _____
- _____

Target date: _____

Key Objective/Responsibility #5:

- _____
- _____
- _____

Target date: _____

Discussion Tool

This tool should be used to prepare for the Performance Appraisal discussion. Following are suggested topics and questions to help manager and employee build a strong working relationship. Feel free to modify them if necessary, or use as is, for your on-going performance communication.

Review Key Objectives/Responsibilities
- What's working; what's not working?
- What barriers do you encounter in meeting your goals?

Communicating Effectively
- How do you prefer to give and receive feedback?
- Are you meeting frequently enough?
- What information do you need to be more effective?
- What do you need to know about each other to work together effectively?

Departmental Obstacles/Strengths
- Are department goals clearly communicated?
- Are department roles clear?

Employee Development and Job Enrichment
- What changes in your skills and abilities would most benefit you and the organization?
- What skills do you need to complete your objectives next year?
- What on-the-job activities would provide greater job satisfaction and achievement of career and personal goals?

Skills and Capabilities

Consider each of the following skills and abilities in evaluating how the Key Objectives/Responsibilities were accomplished:

1. **Results Focused**
   - Looks for and seizes opportunities to do more or to do things better
   - Has a sense of ownership, pride, continuous improvement and urgency about tasks
   - Sees obstacles as "challenges" and enjoys overcoming them
   - Is very bottom-line oriented; steadfastly pushes towards and achieves agreed-upon results
   - Can work effectively within the organization; knows how to get things done

2. **Innovation**
   - Continually thinks "out of the box," and inspires others to do the same
   - Uses good judgment in the evaluation and implementation of creative ideas
   - Analyzes causes of problems, develops alternatives and creative solutions; solves problems quickly
   - Generates and uses creative ideas to improve processes, systems, products, or services

3. **Change Tolerance**
   - Modifies style or approach as appropriate to achieve goals
   - Adjusts easily to changing or unexpected demands at work and changing priorities
   - Handles personal stress; can be counted on to hold things together during difficult times
   - Comfortably handles risk and uncertainty

4. **Customer Satisfaction**
   - Has a clear understanding who customers are (internal and external) within our marketplace
   - Is dedicated to meeting the expectations and requirements of internal and external customers
   - Understands customer needs and uses this information to prioritize what the organization must do to fulfill them; talks and acts with customers in mind

5. **Teamwork**
   - Encourages cooperation, collaboration, and co-ownership of processes
   - Works effectively in groups and creates synergy among groups
   - Works effectively with other departments/divisions across the organization
   - Demonstrates integrity in all actions and decisions

6. **Communication**
   - Communicates clearly and in a timely manner, both orally and in writing
   - Shares information and is open and honest in communications across the organization
   - Engages in productive and constructive debate
   - Maximizes the communications systems and tools that are available

7. **Project Management**
   - Establishes aggressive but realistic goals for self and others
   - Develops plans that support corporate objectives and that provide clear focus
   - Communicates plans and gains input from peers and employees
   - Effectively manages projects and priorities

Additional Competencies for First-Level Managers

8. Leads Courageously

- Makes others feel like important contributors
- Treats others with respect and dignity and is sensitive to their unique needs and to their "motivators"
- Gets others involved so that they feel ownership, empowered, and energized
- Inspires enthusiasm and commitment for the company, its products, and its future success
- Understands and promotes the company's strategy

9. Market Driven

- Exhibits knowledge and understanding of [Company's] marketplace when making decisions
- Continually scans the external environment to evaluate how potential ideas may be used to our advantage
- Recognizes and seizes opportunities for our products and services
- Is skilled at bringing the creative ideas of others to market

10. Develops People

- Nurtures talent from within and coaches for high performance
- Clarifies expectations with people and provides timely and appropriate feedback
- Hires talented people and supports diversity
- Pushes decisions down to the appropriate level

11. Staffing/EEO

- Identifies staffing needs, defines selection criteria, uses effective recruiting methods, and selects top performers in a timely manner who have potential for increased contribution to the company.
- Makes all employment decisions in a timely manner consistent with the principles of applicable laws prohibiting discrimination.

Additional Competencies for Senior-Level Managers

12. Strategic Capability

- Sees ahead clearly; can anticipate future consequences and trends accurately
- Has broad knowledge and perspective; is future oriented; can create competitive and breakthrough strategies and plans
- Deals with concepts and complexity comfortably; described as intellectually sharp, capable, and agile
- Looks toward the broadest possible view of an issue/challenge; thinks globally

13. Command Skills

- Can maneuver through complex political situations effectively
- Can negotiate skillfully in tough situations with both internal and external groups; can be both direct and forceful as well as diplomatic
- Knowledgeable about how the organization functions and how to get things done both through formal channels and the informal network
- Gains support and commitment from others; asserts own ideas and persuades others; mobilizes people to take action

Recommended Performance Appraisal Process

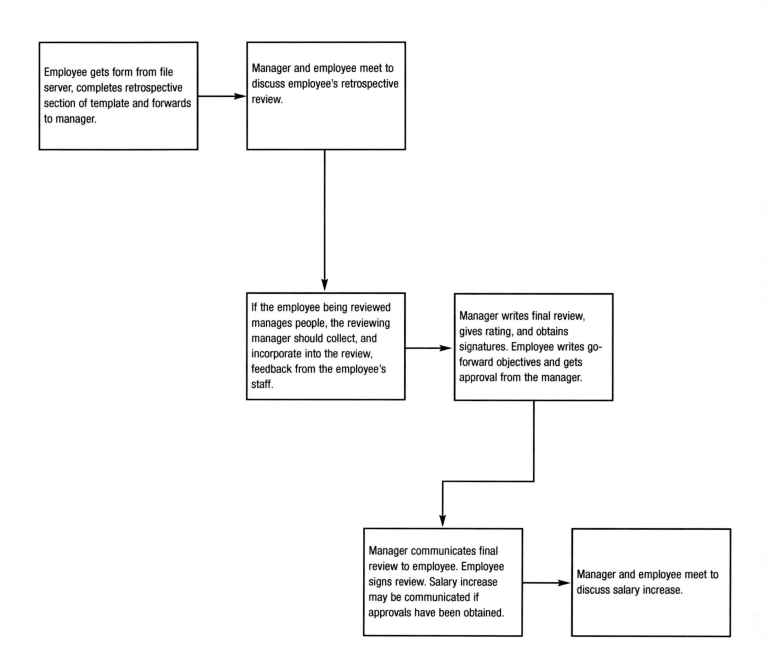

Employee gets form from file server, completes retrospective section of template and forwards to manager.

Manager and employee meet to discuss employee's retrospective review.

If the employee being reviewed manages people, the reviewing manager should collect, and incorporate into the review, feedback from the employee's staff.

Manager writes final review, gives rating, and obtains signatures. Employee writes go-forward objectives and gets approval from the manager.

Manager communicates final review to employee. Employee signs review. Salary increase may be communicated if approvals have been obtained.

Manager and employee meet to discuss salary increase.

Performance Review

Employee's Name: _____   Review Period: _____

Employee's Title: _____   Department: _____

Supervisor/Title: _____   Today's Date: _____

Section I: Desired Overall Results for HR Manager

This position is a part of our management team. It exists so that the organization will have a workplace environment where employees are valued and productive. It provides a helpful resource for managers to use to strategically plan people issues.

The person holding this position produces this end result by effectively designing and administering programs that resolve day to day problems, increase retention, improve recruiting efforts, streamline hiring process, ensure competitive pay and benefit practices.

Employee Perspective   **Manager Perspective**

_____   _____
_____   _____
_____   _____
_____   _____
_____   _____
_____   _____
_____   _____
_____   _____
_____   _____
_____   _____
_____   _____
_____   _____

Goals for Future Performance *(Describe as Continue, Improve,* or New Goals)*

_____
_____
_____
_____
_____
_____
_____
_____
_____
_____
_____
_____
_____

Section II: Demonstrated Support of Core Values

We have established values for all staff to follow. These values are intended to carry us into the future. They serve as the philosophical yardstick against which much of our style and service delivery can be measured. As this person strives to produce the results summarized in section, how have they exhibited these values during this review period?

Employee Perspective

Manager Perspective

_____   _____
_____   _____
_____   _____
_____   _____
_____   _____
_____   _____
_____   _____
_____   _____
_____   _____
_____   _____

Future Goals for Core Values *(Describe as Continue, Improve,* or New Goals)*

_____
_____
_____
_____
_____
_____
_____
_____
_____
_____
_____
_____

Performance-Based Compensation

Total Point Goal _____ (Total cannot exceed 100)

	Description	Maximum Goals
A.		
B.		
C.		
	Total Possible Personal Initiative Points	

Employee Feedback on the Review Process

For the Employee: This performance review is designed for you and your supervisor to discuss your performance. Your feedback is an important part of the discussion. If you have questions or comments about the review, you should write them here and talk to your supervisor about them. You may also use this page to offer suggestions to make your job or work unit more efficient or effective. You should discuss your comments with your supervisor.

❏   My supervisor and I have talked about this review. I have no comments.

❏   My supervisor and I have talked about this review. I would like to offer the following comments.

_____

_____

_____

_____

_____

_____

_____

_____

_____

_____

_____

_____

_____

_____

_____

_____

_____

Employee Signature _____ Date: _____

Supervisor Signature _____ Date: _____

*Performance improvement plan may be required.

Performance Review Guidelines

A performance review gives an employee feedback on how well he/she is doing his/her job. It establishes goals for future performance. This form is designed to help you and the employee focus on the employee's job. It should be completed using the second person (e.g., "You have been on time to work every day over the past year.").

Briefly summarize the **Essential Functions** of the employee's job in the left hand column on the front page. Most jobs have four or five Essential Functions. For instance, the essential functions for an Administrative Assistant might include typing, filing, calendar coordination, monthly reports, and public relations. Briefly describe each of these functions in the left column. Discuss the employee's past performance and future expectations for the employee in the large middle column.

Indicate a future performance goal for each essential function or sub-function by placing a **C** (Continue), **I** (Improve), or **N** (New). **Continue** means the employee is performing the job successfully and should keep doing the job the same way in the future. **Improve** means the employee must correct performance deficiencies or change certain job related behaviors. **New** means the employee's job will change in the upcoming review period and different or more difficult tasks will be assigned.

Corporate Responsibilities are listed on the second page. These are performance factors that are unique or important to this organization. Attendance, safety, and customer relations are examples of corporate responsibilities. You should list the corporate responsibilities that relate to this employee and discuss her/his performance in these areas.

Use **Supervisor's Overall Comments** to summarize the total performance contributions of the employee and provide direction for future performance.

Use the **Objectives for the Next Review Period** section to list your expectations for the employee for the next review period.

Assign an overall rating as follows:

Unacceptable: Means that on an overall basis the employee has, during the review period, performed in a manner significantly below the level to be expected considering the employee's previous experience, tenure in the job, and the employee's duties and responsibilities, *and* that it appears to be reasonably certain that the employee is either unwilling or unable to perform successfully.

Improvement Needed: Means that considering the employee's previous experience, tenure in the job, and job duties and responsibilities, the employee has, during the review period, performed some duties successfully *and* that the employee has the potential for successful performance.

Successful Work: Means that the employee's overall performance, during the review period, has been at or above the level expected considering the employee's previous experience, tenure in the job, and job duties and responsibilities.

Exceptional Work: Means that the employee's overall performance, during the review period, has significantly exceeded expected levels of performance considering the employee's previous experience, tenure in the job, and job duties and responsibilities.

Next, the employee should complete the **Employee Feedback** section of the form. The employee, supervisor, and manager should sign the form. The supervisor should provide the employee with a copy and forward the original to Human Resources.

Employee Performance Review

Employee/Title: _____   Review Period:_____

Supervisor/Title: _____   Today's Date: _____

Major Job Duties Functions	Supervisor Feedback	Goal
1. _____		
_____		
_____		
_____		
2. _____		
_____		
_____		
_____		
3. _____		
_____		
_____		
_____		
4. _____		
_____		
_____		
_____		

Corporate Responsibilities	Supervisor Feedback	Goal
Customer Service: We expect you to make our customers your highest priority. This means that you treat them with courtesy and respect. It means that you help them and respond to their requests in a timely, accurate, and complete manner. It means that you seek help from others when necessary to meet customer needs.	_____	_____
Dependability: We expect you to meet and adhere to deadlines and time schedules. This includes things like project assignments, meeting attendance, responding to correspondence. We expect to be notified when you will be absent or late in a timely manner.	_____	_____

Corporate Responsibilities	Supervisor Feedback	Goal
Safety: We expect you to plan and carry out your work in a safe manner. We expect you to wear required safety gear and clothing; use machines and equipment according to manufacturer's instructions. We expect you to correct and/or report unsafe conditions when you encounter them.		

Overall Feedback	Objectives for Next Review Period

☐ Unacceptable work ☐ Needs development ☐ Successful work ☐ Exceptional work

Employee Feedback

Employee _____   Date: _____

Supervisor _____   Date: _____

Manager _____   Date: _____

F. Supervisor and Management Reviews

The job of a supervisor involves planning, organizing, and other leadership behaviors. Supervisors need to know if they are doing those things correctly. Most organizations use a separate or modified review to be sure that managers provide feedback on those special performance traits. In most cases, the form also provides space for feedback on non-leadership responsibilities.

1. **Performance Appraisal and Development Plan—Year End, Managers:** Lists specific supervisory traits and provides for midyear and year-end evaluation and rating, as well as development objectives, page 139

2. **Management and Executive Annual Performance Appraisal:** Lists leadership and supervisory competencies and provides space for comments and ratings, page 145

Performance Appraisal and Development Plan – Year End, Managers

Employee Name: _____

Employee #: _____

Job Title: _____

Department: _____

Review Period From: _____

Review Period To: _____

Last Appraisal Date: _____

Date of Appraisal: _____

Hire Date: _____

Months in Current Level: _____

Evaluating Supervisor: _____

Next Appraisal Date: _____

This performance appraisal is an important tool in [Company Name's] overall performance management process and employee development. The supervisor should appraise the employee's overall performance primarily on whether the employee's performance produced the desired results in each of the principle accountabilities of the job during this appraisal period. Description terms, such as improving, consistent, and declining, are key in recording accurate performance records.

General Responsibilities – Competencies and/or commitments that employees must demonstrate to perform their jobs. The responsibilities may be weighted. Some areas will have a greater impact than others and should be considered accordingly. The relative value should be discussed with the employee and noted on the form.

Performance Objectives – Expectations selected to be accomplished by a particular date. They are based on goals and objectives identified by department management. They have been identified as being necessary to enhance the functional operations of the individual's area of responsibility for the upcoming performance cycle. Objectives must be measurable.

Ratings are based on the following scale:

1. **Consistently Exceeds Expectations –** The employee consistently exceeds all the expectations for responsibilities and objectives, skills, abilities, and commitment required for the job. Possesses superior knowledge of major aspects of the total job and has had experience in each of these areas. This rating is used as special recognition for extraordinary accomplishments that have significant impact on the organization.

2. **Frequently Exceeds Expectations –** The employee achieves and frequently exceeds expectations for responsibilities and objectives. Demonstrates necessary skills, abilities, and commitment required for the job. Possesses a working knowledge of the major aspects of the total job and has had experience in each of these areas. This rating is for unusually effective employees who perform above what is normally expected.

3. **Meets Expectations –** The employee generally meets established expectations for responsibilities and objectives. Demonstrates required skills, abilities, and commitment for the job. Possesses some knowledge of the major aspects of the job and has had experience in many of these areas. This rating describes the employee whose overall performance is satisfactory, and any minor areas where performance should have been better were counterbalanced by performance beyond expectations.

4. **Almost Attains Expectations –** The employee does not always meet all expectations for responsibilities and objectives identified for area of responsibility. Possess most necessary knowledge, skills, abilities required for the job, but additional training or commitment is required. This rating describes the employee who meets only the very minimum position requirements and whose performance could be improved through development, experience, and/or application.

5. **Below Expectations –** The employee does not meet expectations for responsibilities and objectives. Does not demonstrate necessary knowledge, skills, abilities, and commitment required for the total job. This rating describes the employee who has not kept pace with changing requirements, whose successes have been only occasional, or whose performance has been deteriorating. Immediate and substantial improvement is needed in order to have continued employment. A performance improvement plan needs to be developed.

Section I

Rate each employee on the general responsibilities listed below by placing a rating in the appropriate box. A summary of accomplishments and/or a description of skills and abilities that require improvement or exceeded expectations is required for each area.

	Rating	Weighting	Results
Job Knowledge: Acquires, understands, and applies technical and professional information and skills. Comments: _____ _____ _____			
Organizational Skills: Sets objectives to meet commitments, budgets, forecasts, etc. Organizes work, establishes priorities, makes proper assignments of personnel, and efficient allocation of resources. Comments: _____ _____ _____			
Leadership Skills: Guides individuals or groups to achieve desired results. Delegates by allocating decision making and other responsibilities appropriately and effectively. Develops subordinates by improving their skills and competencies for current and future jobs. Gives performance reviews on time and takes an active role in the development of subordinates. Comments: _____ _____ _____			
Communication Skills: Listens effectively and provides clear, concise, and accurate verbal and written information to groups or individuals in an appropriate and timely manner. Comments: _____ _____ _____			
Safety Management: Ensures all direct reports have been adequately trained in safety. Informs employees of hazards to which they may be exposed. Promptly responds to any employee concerns regarding unsafe working conditions. Accurately completes any required reports related to on the job injuries and illness and forwards reports to the appropriate person in a timely manner. Comments: _____ _____ _____			
Personal Qualities: Possesses good work ethics, drive, energy, and persistence to achieve ambitious goals. Dependable and stable under pressure or opposition adapting to changing, unusual or difficult situations. Effectively interacts with others in the accomplishment of tasks. Gives/accepts constructive criticism; considers diversity and viewpoints of others; cooperates with other employees in a pleasant and courteous manner. Handles difficult situations in a tactful manner. Comments: _____ _____ _____			

Overall Performance Factor Rating: _____ %

Section II Performance and Personal Development Objectives for the Current Appraisal Period

List specific job assignments and responsibilities pertaining to a particular job function, including performance and personal development objectives outlined in the previous performance and appraisal plan, if applicable. A summary of accomplishments and/or a description of skills and abilities that require improvement is required for each area.

		Rating	Weighting	Results
Goal:				
Comments: _____				
Goal:				
Comments: _____				
Goal:				
Comments: _____				
Goal:				
Comments: _____				
Goal:				
Comments: _____				
Goal:				
Comments: _____				

Overall Objectives Rating: _____ %

Section III   Performance Summary

Considering evaluations in Section I and II, the overall performance can be summarized as follows: _____

_____

_____

_____

Section IV   Employee's Expressed Short- and Long-Term Goals

_____

_____

_____

Section V   Employee Comments

_____

_____

_____

Section VI   Rating Summary

	Rating	Weighting	Results
General Responsibilities (Performance Factors)		100%	
Performance and Personal Development Objectives /Current Year Final Rating		0%	
Total Combined Performance Rating		100%	

Section VII   Performance Plan Acceptance

I have read and discussed the contents of the appraisal with my supervisor.

Employee's Signature: _____   Date: _____
Note: Your signature does not indicate that you agree with the comments or ratings.

Supervisor's Signature: _____   Date: _____

2nd Level Supervisor's Signature: _____   Date: _____

General Manager's Signature: _____   Date: _____

Human Resources Signature: _____   Date: _____

Section VIII   Performance and Personal Development Objectives for the Next Appraisal Period

List expectations selected for accomplishment by a particular date. They should be based on the departmental goals and objectives and are necessary to enhance the functional operations of the individual's area of responsibility for the upcoming performance cycle. Also list individual development objectives identified by the manager and/or employee needed to improve the technical competence or commitment to perform the job including, organizational skills, decision making skills, leadership skills, communication skills, and personal qualities. Identify specific, measurable actions the employee may take in areas needing improvement. These objectives become the Performance Appraisal and Development Objectives for the next appraisal cycle.

Weighting

Objective

_____   _____

_____

Tentative Timetable: _____

Weighting

Objective

_____   _____

_____

Tentative Timetable: _____

Weighting

Objective

_____   _____

_____

Tentative Timetable: _____

Weighting

Objective

_____   _____

_____

Tentative Timetable: _____

Weighting

Objective

_____   _____

_____

Tentative Timetable: _____

Overall Objectives Weighting: _____%

Management and Executive Annual Performance Appraisal

Employee Name: _____   Appraiser's Name: _____

Employee Title: _____   Department: _____

Appraisal Period:_____

Part I. Competency Evaluation – How This Employee Achieved Results

Ratings for competencies evaluate the degree to which employees used their skills and knowledge in achieving results. While comments are only **mandatory** for competencies evaluated as *Does Not Meet Expectations* or *Exceeds Expectations,* managers are encouraged to substantiate all ratings by commenting on each competency.

Core Competencies

Assess *all* employees on each of the competencies listed in this section by placing the appropriate rating (N, M, or E) in the "Rating" column.

N: Does Not Meet Expectations   **M:** Meets Expectations   **E:** Exceeds Expectations

Competency	Comments	Rating
Strategic Leadership Able to inspire, influence, and enable others to achieve a specific mission. Drive for results/initiative.		
Business and Organization Knowledge Having a solid knowledge of [Company's] businesses and organization as well as the [Industry Name] industry. Ability to identify and learn new information.		
Decision Making Acts on and makes timely decisions with business direction. Delegates decision-making authority to level with capability and information closest to the internal or external customer.		
Customer Focus Ability to anticipate and meet internal/external customer needs in timely manner. Ensures customer satisfaction through process of monitoring, developing, improving, and delivering excellence in products and service.		
Selection and Development of People Competence can be seen by how well self and others are developed.		
Teamwork/Partnering Builds winning teams. Works effectively with others to accomplish goals/resolve problems.		

Core Competencies *continued*

Assess *all* employees on each of the competencies listed in this section by placing the appropriate rating (N, M, or E) in the "Rating" column.

N: Does Not Meet Expectations   **M:** Meets Expectations   **E:** Exceeds Expectations

Competency	Comments	Rating
Accountability Makes aggressive commitments and is willing to be judged against them. Trustworthy with unyielding integrity.		
Vision/Direction Setting Ability to provide clear sense of direction for organization/department. Secures relevant information. Identifies key issues and sets priorities.		
Drive for Results/Resource Management Identifies new ways to improve quality, productivity and customer service. Maximizes talents and abilities. Uses available resources efficiently (e.g., time, materials).		
Adaptability Ability to be flexible when changes occur. Able to anticipate and bring about change when needed.		

Overall Evaluation of Competencies

Please assign an overall rating for the competencies described above by placing an "X" in the appropriate box. You may assign only one rating.

Does Not Meet Expectations	Meets Expectations	Exceeds Expectations

Part II. Summary of Results Achieved for [Year]

Describe specific goals and results achieved during the year and assign a rating in the spaces below.

Performance Goal	Results Achieved	Rating

Appraiser's Comments

The appraiser should provide any additional comments that he/she believes are important for describing the employee's performance and contributions, including any factors that may have positively or adversely impacted performance.

Overall Performance Rating

Please assign an overall performance rating for this employee, taking into consideration both the results that were achieved as well as the means by which they were accomplished (competency evaluations). Select only **one** of the ratings listed below by placing an "X" next to the number that corresponds to your overall evaluation.

_____	5	**Employee Whose Performance Greatly Exceeds Expectations:** This employee consistently exceeds performance expectations while demonstrating a high level of proficiency in all or most of the competencies required in his/her job.
_____	4	**Employee Whose Performance Exceeds Expectations:** This employee consistently meets and frequently exceeds performance expectations while demonstrating a high level of proficiency in many of the competencies required in his/her job.
_____	3	**Employee Whose Performance Meets Expectations:** This employee consistently meets and may occasionally exceed performance expectations while demonstrating proficiency in the competencies required in his/her job.
_____	2	**Employee Whose Performance Does Not Consistently Meet Expectations:** This employee does not consistently meet performance expectations and/or demonstrates only a moderate level of proficiency in the competencies required in his/her job.
_____	1	**Employee Whose Performance Fails To Meet Expectations:** This employee usually fails to meet performance expectations and/or demonstrates only a minimal level of proficiency in the competencies required in his/her job.

Part III. Goal Setting and Annual Performance Planning for [Year]:

Instructions: This section should be completed jointly between appraiser and appraisee. Indicate specific goals and objectives to be accomplished during the forthcoming year.

Overall Goal (What) _____

_____

_____

_____

Specific Performance Objectives (Action Steps)_____

_____

_____

_____

Outcome Measures (Results) _____

_____

_____

_____

Importance of Goal _____

_____

_____

_____

Time of Goal (Target Completion Quarter) _____

_____

_____

_____

Comments _____

_____

_____

_____

Part IV. Signatures

The employee should sign below to acknowledge having received this appraisal and having the opportunity to discuss its contents with the appraiser. Signing does not indicate agreement with the contents of this appraisal, and the employee may comment as appropriate.

_____   _____
Employee's Signature (required)   Date

_____   _____
Appraiser's Signature (required)   Date

_____   _____
Second Appraiser's Signature (include only if necessary, e.g., a dual reporting relationship)   Date

Signature of Reviewer (Appraiser's Immediate Superior)

Your signature below certifies that you have reviewed this appraisal and the comments made by the individual being appraised.

_____   _____
Reviewer's Signature   Date

_____
Title, Department

Comments By Individual Being Appraised

In the space below, please write any comments you have about this appraisal of your performance. Attach additional pages as necessary.

G. Upward Reviews

Traditionally, the focus has been on supervisors evaluating employees. Some organizations have learned that it is just as important for employees to give their supervisors feedback on their leadership and coaching skills. Many supervisors indicate that they value such feedback. Others find it very difficult to accept.

1. **Employee Review of Work Group Leader:** Provides thirteen categories for employee feedback, page 153

2. **Upward Evaluation Report:** Provides twenty categories plus an overall open comments section, page 155

Employee Review of Work Group Leader

Work Group Leader: _____   Title: _____

Today's Date: _____   Due to Human Resources: _____

Instructions: This form is designed to help you give your supervisor feedback on how he/she is doing. It is not necessary for you to sign the form. Once you complete it, you should send it to Human Resources. HR will summarize the feedback from your work group. The summary will be given to your supervisor and his or her supervisor. Your supervisor may decide to meet with your group to discuss the feedback. As you answer the questions, please be as specific as possible. Be honest. Be constructive. Thank you for taking time to give your feedback.

Performance Factors

	Never	Seldom	Occasionally	Frequently	Always
My work group leader's words and actions are consistent. Examples:	❑	❑	❑	❑	❑
My work group leader has a positive affect on morale and attendance. Examples:	❑	❑	❑	❑	❑
My work group leader's management style is comfortable for our group. Examples:	❑	❑	❑	❑	❑
My work group leader tells us about company and department changes. Examples:	❑	❑	❑	❑	❑
My work group leader listens carefully. Examples:	❑	❑	❑	❑	❑
My work group leader communicates our needs to upper management. Examples:	❑	❑	❑	❑	❑
My work group leader asks for input and ideas. Examples:	❑	❑	❑	❑	❑

Performance Factors *continued*

My work group leader sets and follows clear priorities.	**Never**	**Seldom**	**Occasionally**	**Frequently**	**Always**
Examples: _____	❏	❏	❏	❏	❏

_____

_____

_____

My work group leader encourages me to make decisions and supports me.	**Never**	**Seldom**	**Occasionally**	**Frequently**	**Always**
Examples: _____	❏	❏	❏	❏	❏

_____

_____

_____

My work group leader encourages me and helps me to grow and develop on the job.	**Never**	**Seldom**	**Occasionally**	**Frequently**	**Always**
Examples: _____	❏	❏	❏	❏	❏

_____

_____

_____

Upward Evaluation Report

Name _____   Date _____

Answer the following questions concerning the above individual.

Complete this evaluation on anyone who has served as your supervisor in any significant manner in the past year. When you complete this evaluation including comments, please run a copy and mail to [Staff Member], Director of Human Resources in Administration as soon as you can, no later than [Date]. All reports will be shared confidentially and privately with those evaluated.

1. **Does the supervisor set a good example in his/her work habits?**

   ❑ Always   ❑ Usually   ❑ Sometimes   ❑ Rarely   ❑ Never

2. **Is the supervisor approachable and available when needed?**

   ❑ Always   ❑ Usually   ❑ Sometimes   ❑ Rarely   ❑ Never

3. **When you are assigned new duties and responsibilities by the supervisor, how are they explained?**

   ❑ Well explained   ❑ Adequately   ❑ Partially   ❑ Not satisfactorily

4. **When the supervisor makes changes in the work you had done, are you told the reason for the change?**

   ❑ Always   ❑ Usually   ❑ Sometimes   ❑ Rarely   ❑ Never

5. **Does the supervisor make you feel that you were important to the success of the engagement?**

   ❑ Always   ❑ Usually   ❑ Sometimes   ❑ Rarely   ❑ Never

6. **Does the supervisor assign significant tasks to expand skills and experience?**

   ❑ Always   ❑ Usually   ❑ Sometimes   ❑ Rarely   ❑ Never

7. **What degree of on-the-job training do you receive from the supervisor?**

   ❑ A great deal   ❑ A substantial amount   ❑ Some   ❑ Very little   ❑ None

8. **Does the supervisor publicly give credit for the success of a project to the employees who contributed to it?**

   ❑ Always   ❑ Usually   ❑ Sometimes   ❑ Rarely   ❑ Never

9. **Do you feel that favoritism is shown by the supervisor?**

   ❑ None   ❑ Very little   ❑ Some   ❑ Much

10. **Does the supervisor on the engagement or project keep you informed on plans and progress?**

    ❑ Always   ❑ Usually   ❑ Sometimes   ❑ Rarely   ❑ Never

11. **When you are assigned to work on the engagement or the project with the supervisor, do you find him/her to be receptive to ideas and suggestions for new or better ways of doing things?**

    ❑ Always   ❑ Usually   ❑ Sometimes   ❑ Rarely   ❑ Never

12. **Does the supervisor build trust by openly sharing information?**

    ❑ Always   ❑ Usually   ❑ Sometimes   ❑ Rarely   ❑ Never

13. **Does the supervisor invite you to participate in the planning of engagements or projects?**

    ❑ Always   ❑ Usually   ❑ Sometimes   ❑ Rarely   ❑ Never

14. **Are you allowed a sufficient degree of self-management?**

 ❏ Always   ❏ Usually   ❏ Sometimes   ❏ Rarely   ❏ Never

15. **Is criticism expressed constructively and in a professional manner?**

 ❏ Always   ❏ Usually   ❏ Sometimes   ❏ Rarely   ❏ Never

16. **Does the supervisor cope well with frustrations, pressures, and setbacks?**

 ❏ Always   ❏ Usually   ❏ Sometimes   ❏ Rarely   ❏ Never

17. **Does the supervisor respond nondefensively to criticism and challenges to his/her viewpoint?**

 ❏ Always   ❏ Usually   ❏ Sometimes   ❏ Rarely   ❏ Never

18. **Does the supervisor set reasonable goals?**

 ❏ Always   ❏ Usually   ❏ Sometimes   ❏ Rarely   ❏ Never

19. **Does the supervisor emphasize cooperation instead of competitiveness within the work group?**

 ❏ Always   ❏ Usually   ❏ Sometimes   ❏ Rarely   ❏ Never

20. **Does the supervisor give due consideration to your input, ideas, and suggestions?**

 ❏ Always   ❏ Usually   ❏ Sometimes   ❏ Rarely   ❏ Never

Use the space below to make comments that will be useful to the person you are upwardly evaluating. If you are able, provide specific examples of indications of strength, areas of concern, and any suggestions for improvement.

Comments: _____

_____

_____

_____

_____

_____

_____

_____

_____

_____

_____

_____

_____

_____

_____

_____

_____

_____

_____

_____

H. 360-Degree Reviews

There is much more to doing a job than sitting at a desk or standing at a machine. Virtually every occupation involves interacting with co-workers, customers, vendors, or suppliers. The 360-degree review provides a method for gathering and considering input from a variety of people who interact with the employee.

1. **Employee Peer Review:** Asks generic questions, requests a rating and specific examples, and asks for feedback on open-ended areas of strengths and weaknesses, page 159

2. **360-degree Feedback Tool:** Provides numerous job traits and asks for rating on a five-point scale, page 161

3. **360 Survey: Executive Level:** Focuses on leadership and decision making for senior-level leaders, page 167

4. **Staff Development and Performance Evaluation Team Member Review:** Has a questionnaire format to give supervisor input from employee constituents, page 173

Employee Peer Review

Employee to be rated: _____   Name: _____

Purpose: *The primary goals of the Employee Peer Review are to measure skills that help company productivity and to provide constructive feedback for improved performance. Your input is valuable since results of this review will be integrated into each person's overall performance evaluation. We make every effort to maintain the confidentiality of this information. However, it is possible that the person being evaluated will be able to identify the source from the nature of specific examples.*

Please respond to those questions that you feel qualified to answer. Feel free to add comments.

	Yes, definitely	Somewhat	No, not much
Will s/he volunteer to help you or others when a need is identified? Will s/he help to train new people when the opportunity arises?	❑	❑	❑

Give specific examples: _____

_____

_____

	Yes, definitely	Somewhat	No, not much
Does s/he share ideas and suggestions with you and/or others?	❑	❑	❑

Give specific examples: _____

_____

_____

	Yes, definitely	Somewhat	No, not much
Does s/he contribute to solving problems in your and/or other areas? If a problem develops in another area that affects him/her, will this person assist in solving it (rather than complaining or feeling frustrated)?	❑	❑	❑

Give specific examples: _____

_____

_____

	To a great extent	Somewhat beyond the norm	About enough to get by
Overall, to what degree do you believe this person contributes his/her skills, talents, energy, and ideas to help the company be as successful as possible in all areas?	❑	❑	❑

Give specific examples: _____

_____

_____

To what degree does this person contribute to the overall success of the team, department, or company? _____

_____

_____

_____

_____

In what area(s) does the employee perform particularly well? _____

_____

_____

_____

_____

In what area(s) should the employee focus his/her development (talents and/or weaknesses)? _____

_____

_____

_____

_____

Additional comments: _____

_____

_____

_____

_____

_____

_____

_____

_____

360-degree Feedback Tool

Dear _____,

I am currently working on a career development plan. Feedback from others is an important part of that process. I value your opinion and appreciate your taking the time to help me determine my strengths, as well as my opportunities for development.

The attached feedback form will take approximately 10–20 minutes to complete. When rating each area, please think of my performance or behavior in a work setting.

Please be as objective and honest as you can in completing this form.

Thank you,

_____ Date Sent:_____

Instructions To Rater:

1. Read the description for each competency area below. Consider what you've observed in this person in the past, and select the rating that best describes his/her level of performance or behavior in that area overall.

    - *Significant Improvement Needed* — Still has much to learn, or is particularly weak in this area.

    - *Slight Improvement Needed* — Still has some learning to do, or could/should be better in this area already.

    - *Skilled/Competent* — Demonstrates most aspects of this competency most of the time.

    - *Particularly Talented* — Is recognized for strength in this area; e.g., is chosen for projects or assignments based on the skills s/he brings in this competency.

    - *Outstanding/Role Model* — Is recognized as a leader in this competency; frequently teaches others how to do it well.

    - *Not Applicable/Not Observed* — Don't know how the person performs or behaves in a particular area, or the person is not yet in a role requiring this competency.

2. Comments/qualifiers should be included at the end of the section to which they apply. When possible, include specific examples of situations or observed behavior relevant to your comments.

3. Be honest and objective in your assessment, to ensure the right areas will be addressed. We make every effort to maintain the confidentiality of this information; in general, only consolidated feedback will be shared with the individual. However, it is possible that the person being evaluated will be able to identify the source of the information from the nature of the comments.

4. Return the completed form to Human Resources in the envelope provided. Make sure the name of the person you are rating is written on the first page of the form.

5. Please complete this assessment within one week of the "Date Sent" listed above.

Name of person being assessed:_____

Your relationship: ❏ Self Assessment   ❏ Manager/Supervisor   ❏ Peer   ❏ Person Who Reports to Person Being Assessed   ❏ Client

Strategic/Execution Factor	Significant Improvement Needed	Slight Improvement Needed	Skilled/ Competent	Particularly Talented	Outstanding/ Role Model	Not Applicable/ Not Observed
Surpasses Client Expectations Impresses clients with exceptional service; continually searches for ways to improve service and quality of work; understands and anticipates client needs, wants, and issues; incorporates client needs and requirements into services; ensures client issues are successfully resolved; ensures quality standards are understood and executed by all on team.	1	2	3	4	5	0
Knows the Business Understands all significant aspects of the public accounting business and specifically of the [Company] operation; keeps up-to-date on new rules, regulations, and procedures; understands the work performed in different areas of the organization and how major practice areas interrelate (generalist knowledge); maintains in-depth (specialist) knowledge in one of the major practice areas: [List of Practice Areas]; serves as conduit from client to [Company's] entire knowledge database and people resources.	1	2	3	4	5	0

Comments: _____
_____
_____

Administrative Factor	Significant Improvement Needed	Slight Improvement Needed	Skilled/ Competent	Particularly Talented	Outstanding/ Role Model	Not Applicable/ Not Observed
Works Efficiently Makes efficient use of time; sets and maintains priorities for own work; plans own work and schedules activities so that deadlines and objectives are met; balances time and attention given to multiple demands and competing priorities; attends to details while remaining focused on the big picture; focuses on important information without getting bogged down in details; applies and enforces effective meeting norms; evaluates current methods and constantly looks for new and better ways of doing things.	1	2	3	4	5	0
Delegates Effectively Directs the activities of individuals and groups toward the accomplishment of goals; delegates accountabilities and assignments to lowest possible level; clearly communicates assignments and expectations; monitors progress on assignments and redirects efforts as needed.	1	2	3	4	5	0
Leverages Technology Maintains leading edge literacy in the technologies available; utilizes electronic media to enhance own and others' productivity, knowledge, and communication; understands and is comfortable with technology as tools, never barriers, to producing results; coaches others to utilize media to fullest potential.	1	2	3	4	5	0

Comments: _____
_____
_____

Interpersonal Factor	Significant Improvement Needed	Slight Improvement Needed	Skilled/ Competent	Particularly Talented	Outstanding/ Role Model	Not Applicable/ Not Observed
Communicates Effectively Promptly and consistently shares relevant information with others; makes sure people have no "surprises;" listens carefully to others on all levels (verbal/nonverbal); clarifies what people say to ensure understanding; speaks clearly, concisely, and expressively; writes clearly, concisely, and expressively; comprehends and appropriately applies written information to situations and problems.	1	2	3	4	5	0
Builds Relationships Relates to all people in an open, friendly, and accepting manner; shows sincere interest in others and their concerns; works well with others to achieve common goals; takes initiative to assist clients and coworkers and address their questions and concerns; treats others fairly and consistently; maintains active, profiled involvement with professional and community service organizations.	1	2	3	4	5	0
Supports Teamwork Considers the needs and capabilities of others when working together; plays different roles based on needs of team; ensures that the collective resources of teams are utilized optimally; encourages team members to collaborate; involves others in shaping plans and decisions that affect them.	1	2	3	4	5	0

Comments: _____

_____

_____

Self-Management Factor	Significant Improvement Needed	Slight Improvement Needed	Skilled/ Competent	Particularly Talented	Outstanding/ Role Model	Not Applicable/ Not Observed
Demonstrates Adaptability Adjusts readily to multiple demands, shifting priorities, change, and unexpected events; remains calm, effective, and even-tempered in high pressure circumstances; maintains composure in the face of criticism, conflict, or hostility; projects a positive and cheerful outlook; rebounds quickly from setbacks and disappointments; understands own limitations and strengths.	1	2	3	4	5	0
Drives for Results Accepts responsibility and ownership for own performance and that of the team; establishes challenging goals and works hard to achieve them; volunteers to take on additional responsibility; works diligently toward the accomplishment of goals or assignments even if unpleasant or routine; persists in the face of obstacles; identifies what needs to be done and does it; works effectively with minimal direction or feedback; willingly makes own decisions.	1	2	3	4	5	0
Learns Continually Understands limits of own knowledge and capability; reads continually (journals, industry publications, books, Internet) to keep abreast of developments in the profession; maintains diverse interests to support creative approaches to business problems and business growth.	1	2	3	4	5	0

Self-Management Factor continued

	Significant Improvement Needed	Slight Improvement Needed	Skilled/ Competent	Particularly Talented	Outstanding/ Role Model	Not Applicable/ Not Observed
Acts With Integrity Behaves in a manner consistent with expressed values and ethical principles; builds trust with others by demonstrating consistency between words and actions; follows through on commitments; models [Company's] values through actions; follows established procedures, rules, and policies; puts aside personal feelings and preferences when conducting business or assigning work.	1	2	3	4	5	0

Comments: _____

_____

_____

Entrepreneurial Factor

	Significant Improvement Needed	Slight Improvement Needed	Skilled/ Competent	Particularly Talented	Outstanding/ Role Model	Not Applicable/ Not Observed
Thinks Like An Owner Forward thinking, creative, and innovative; identifies and acts on cross-selling opportunities and directs appropriate resources to capitalize on such; balances client and [Company] needs in interactions/transactions; seeks out new business opportunities; assesses risk factors in business situations and takes action quickly as appropriate; consults with other stakeholders on critical issues but maintains decision focus; understands how to maximize the profitability of the business; represents the organization publicly in a positive and professional manner, even under difficult circumstances.	1	2	3	4	5	0
Addresses Issues Quickly determines when deviations or anomalies can lead to problems; anticipates problems and issues; systematically identifies causes of problems; proactively seeks information to assess client needs; generates and evaluates alternative solutions; solves problems/meets needs quickly and effectively; builds consensus; works toward win/win, value-added solutions whenever possible.	1	2	3	4	5	0

Comments: _____

_____

_____

Leadership Factor

	Significant Improvement Needed	Slight Improvement Needed	Skilled/ Competent	Particularly Talented	Outstanding/ Role Model	Not Applicable/ Not Observed
Coaches Others Facilitates the development of others; sets clear goals, standards, and guidelines; provides timely, constructive feedback; takes appropriate action with problem performers in a timely way; assigns challenging assignments to develop the skills of staff; supports employee development efforts; seeks alternative viewpoints; involves others in making decisions that affect them.	1	2	3	4	5	0

Leadership Factor continued	Significant Improvement Needed	Slight Improvement Needed	Skilled/ Competent	Particularly Talented	Outstanding/ Role Model	Not Applicable/ Not Observed
Inspires Others Encourages others to consistently meet and exceed performance goals with enthusiasm; inspires others to work at peak performance; adapts motivational strategy to individual needs; creates an enjoyable work environment to maximize retention of staff; recognizes and rewards the accomplishments of individuals and the team; creates excitement and energy among team that is visible to the clients; focuses employees on satisfying clients.	1	2	3	4	5	0

Comments: _____

_____

_____

360 Survey: Executive Level

Name of person you are assessing:_____

You are this person's (please check one):

❑ **Manager;** direct supervisor of this person.

❑ **Direct Report;** you report to this person; he/she is your supervisor.

❑ **Coworker;** a peer of this person; report to same manager.

❑ **Customer;** a key internal client of this person.

❑ **Self;** you are the person named above.

The above named person is participating in [Company's] 360 Survey. This questionnaire survey is a constructive way to help leaders discover their strengths, as well as areas for further development regarding **the behavioral competencies of their position.**

We make every effort to maintain the confidentiality of this information. [Outside Consultant] will not share the raw results of this survey with anyone. Your answers to the items will be combined and averaged with other responses in the report and/or graph form presented to the above-named person. However, it is possible that the person being evaluated will be able to identify the source of the information from the nature of the comments.

The only person whose identity will be known as a respondent is the manager, as there is usually only one person in that category. Thus, both their numeric and narrative responses will be attributable. The individual numeric and narrative responses of direct reports, coworkers/peers, and customers will be identified within a category format but the name is never identified.

Your candid responses to the survey items are valued and appreciated. Thank you for your participation.

Please complete this survey no later than _____.

Instructions: How satisfied are you with the way this person...

For the scalar questions, please select **one** response using the following scale:

1 = Highly Dissatisfied	3 = Moderately Satisfied	5 = Highly Satisfied
2 = Dissatisfied	4 = Satisfied	N/A = Not Applicable, does not apply

Competency: Leading Through Vision and Values

1. Helps others understand the organization's vision and values and their importance?   1   2   3   4   5   N/A

2. Translates the vision and values into day-to-day activities and behaviors; guides and motivates others to take actions that support the vision and values?   1   2   3   4   5   N/A

3. Takes actions, makes decisions, and shapes team or group priorities to reflect the organization's vision and values?   1   2   3   4   5   N/A

   Comments: (Please provide comments on your observations of this person's behavior as defined above.)_____

   _____

   _____

Competency: Strategic Decision Making

4. Organizes information and data to identify/explain major trends, problems, and causes; compares and combines information to identify underlying issues?   1   2   3   4   5   N/A

5. Generates and considers options for actions to achieve a long-range goal or vision; develops decision criteria considering factors such as cost, benefits, risks, timing, and buy-in; selects the strategy most likely to succeed?   1   2   3   4   5   N/A

6. Makes sure strategies are carried out; monitors results and makes adjustments as needed?   1   2   3   4   5   N/A

   Comments: (Please provide comments on your observations of this person's behavior as defined by this competency.)_____

   _____

   _____

Competency: Building Partnerships

7. Analyzes the organization and own area to identify key relationships that should be initiated or improved to further the attainment of own area's goals?   1   2   3   4   5   N/A

8. Exchanges information with potential partner areas to clarify partnership benefits and potential problems; collaboratively determines the scope and expectations of the partnership so that both areas' needs can be met?   1   2   3   4   5   N/A

9. Places higher priority on organization's goals than on own area's goals; anticipates effects of own area's actions and decisions on partners; influences others to support partnership objectives?   1   2   3   4   5   N/A

   Comments: (Please provide comments on your observations of this person's behavior as defined by this competency.)_____

   _____

   _____

Competency: **Building Trust**

10. Demonstrates honesty; keeps commitments; behaves in a consistent manner?   1   2   3   4   5   N/A

11. Listens to others and objectively considers others' ideas and opinions, even when they conflict with one's own?   1   2   3   4   5   N/A

12. Treats people with dignity, respect, and fairness; gives proper credit to others; stands up for deserving others and their ideas even in the face of resistance or challenge?   1   2   3   4   5   N/A

Comments: (Please provide comments on your observations of this person's behavior as defined by this competency.)_____

_____

_____

Competency: **Gaining Commitment**

13. Describes expectations, goals, requests, or future states in a way that provides clarity and excites interest?   1   2   3   4   5   N/A

14. Presents own ideas; seeks and develops suggestions of others; makes procedural suggestions?   1   2   3   4   5   N/A

15. Uses appropriate influence strategies to gain genuine agreement; persists by using different approaches as needed to gain commitment?   1   2   3   4   5   N/A

Comments: (Please provide comments on your observations of this person's behavior as defined by this competency.)_____

_____

_____

Competency: **Facilitating Change**

16. Encourages associates to question established work processes or assumptions; challenges associates to ask "why" until underlying cause is discovered; involves stakeholders in continuous improvement actions and alternatives?   1   2   3   4   5   N/A

17. Consistently remains open to ideas offered by others; supports and uses good ideas to solve problems or address issues?   1   2   3   4   5   N/A

18. Helps individuals overcome resistance to change; shows empathy with people who feel loss as a result of change?   1   2   3   4   5   N/A

Comments: (Please provide comments on your observations of this person's behavior as defined by this competency.)_____

_____

_____

Competency: Innovation

19. Identifies implicit assumptions in the way problems or situations are defined or presented; sees   **1   2   3   4   5   N/A**
alternative ways to view or define problems; is not constrained by the thoughts or approaches of others?

20. Combines ideas in unique ways or makes connections between disparate ideas; explores different lines   **1   2   3   4   5   N/A**
of thought; views situations from multiple perspectives; brainstorms multiple approaches/solutions?

21. Targets important areas for innovation and develops solutions that address meaningful work issues?   **1   2   3   4   5   N/A**

Comments: (Please provide comments on your observations of this person's behavior as defined by this competency.)_____

_____

_____

Competency: Accountability for Results

22. Establishes criteria and/or work procedures to achieve a high level of quality, productivity, or service?   **1   2   3   4   5   N/A**

23. Dedicates required time and energy to assignments or tasks to ensure that no aspect of the work   **1   2   3   4   5   N/A**
is neglected; works to overcome obstacles to completing tasks or assignments?

24. Accepts responsibility for outcomes (positive or negative) of one's work; admits mistakes and refocuses   **1   2   3   4   5   N/A**
efforts when appropriate?

25. Provides encouragement and support to others in accepting responsibility; does not accept others'   **1   2   3   4   5   N/A**
denial of responsibility without questioning?

Comments: (Please provide comments on your observations of this person's behavior as defined by this competency.)_____

_____

_____

Competency: Building Collaborative Working Relationships

26. Proactively tries to build effective working relationships with other people?   **1   2   3   4   5   N/A**

27. Probes for and provides information to clarify situations?   **1   2   3   4   5   N/A**

28. Seeks and expands on original ideas, enhances others' ideas, and contributes own ideas about   **1   2   3   4   5   N/A**
issues at hand?

29. Places higher priority on team or organization goals than on own goals?   **1   2   3   4   5   N/A**

30. Gains agreement from partners to support ideas or take partnership-oriented action; uses sound   **1   2   3   4   5   N/A**
rationale to explain value of actions?

31. Establishes good interpersonal relationships by helping people feel valued, appreciated, and included   **1   2   3   4   5   N/A**
in discussions?

Comments: (Please provide comments on your observations of this person's behavior as defined by this competency.)_____

_____

_____

Competency: **Customer Focus**

32. Actively seeks information to understand customers' circumstances, problems, expectations, and needs?　　1　2　3　4　5　N/A

33. Shares information with customers to build their understanding of issues and capabilities?　　1　2　3　4　5　N/A

34. Builds rapport and cooperative relationships with customers?　　1　2　3　4　5　N/A

35. Considers how actions or plans will affect customers; responds quickly to meet customer needs and resolve problems; avoids overcommitments?　　1　2　3　4　5　N/A

36. Implements effective ways to monitor and evaluate customer concerns, issues, and satisfaction and to anticipate customer needs?　　1　2　3　4　5　N/A

   Comments: (Please provide comments on your observations of this person's behavior as defined by this competency.)_____

   _____

   _____

Competency: **Information-Driven Decision Making**

37. Recognizes issues, problems, or opportunities and determines whether action is needed?　　1　2　3　4　5　N/A

38. Identifies the need for and collects information to better understand issues, problems, and opportunities?　　1　2　3　4　5　N/A

39. Integrates information from a variety of sources; detects trends, associations, and cause-effect relationships?　　1　2　3　4　5　N/A

40. Creates relevant options for addressing problems/opportunities and achieving desired outcomes?　　1　2　3　4　5　N/A

41. Formulates clear decision criteria; evaluates options by considering implications and consequences; chooses an effective option?　　1　2　3　4　5　N/A

42. Implements decisions or initiates actions within a reasonable time?　　1　2　3　4　5　N/A

43. Includes others in the decision-making process as warranted to obtain good information, makes the most appropriate decisions, and ensures buy-in and understanding of the resulting decisions?　　1　2　3　4　5　N/A

   Comments: (Please provide comments on your observations of this person's behavior as defined by this competency.)_____

   _____

   _____

Competency: **Continuous Learning**

44. Seeks and uses feedback and other sources of information to identify appropriate areas for learning?　　1　2　3　4　5　N/A

45. Identifies and participates in appropriate learning activities (e.g., courses, reading, self-study, coaching, experiential learning) that help fulfill learning needs?　　1　2　3　4　5　N/A

46. Actively participates in learning activities in a way that makes the most of the learning experience (e.g., takes notes, asks questions, critically analyzes information, keeps on-the-job application in mind, does required tasks)?　　1　2　3　4　5　N/A

Competency: **Continuous Learning continued**

47. Puts new knowledge, understanding, or skills to practical use on the job; furthers learning through trial and error?   1   2   3   4   5   N/A

48. Puts self in unfamiliar or uncomfortable situations in order to learn; asks questions at the risk of appearing foolish; takes on challenging or unfamiliar assignments?   1   2   3   4   5   N/A

Comments: (Please provide comments on your observations of this person's behavior as defined by this competency.)_____

_____

_____

Competency: **Technical/Professional Knowledge Skills**

49. Understands the technical language of the job?   1   2   3   4   5   N/A

50. Understands what the results of a task, function, or process should be?   1   2   3   4   5   N/A

51. Performs technical or specialized work?   1   2   3   4   5   N/A

52. Stays aware of current developments and trends in all relevant technical/professional knowledge areas?   1   2   3   4   5   N/A

Comments: (Please provide comments on your observations of this person's behavior as defined by this competency.)_____

_____

_____

Comments

It is important that you complete the comment section. Please take a few moments to help this individual understand those things that are most important to you. To ensure anonymity, please avoid comments, phrases, or references that might identify you. These comments will be reported to the person exactly as stated.

Strengths:

53. If you were this leader's coach, what would you tell him/her are his/her **most effective** leadership qualities and behaviors? _____

_____

_____

_____

Improvement Priority:

54. If you were this leader's coach, what specific leadership qualities and behaviors would you encourage him/her to **improve**? _____

_____

_____

_____

Thank you for your honest and considered responses.

Staff Development and Performance Evaluation
Team Member Review

This review is for: _____

Please return this form as soon as possible to: _____

To help me develop a more complete picture of your team member please take a few minutes to complete the questionnaire below. Add any constructive comments you wish to make in the space provided. <u>Please treat the completed form confidentially</u>.

VALUES

Customer Service	Are customers welcomed, kept updated, helped on time, and thanked by this staff member?	❑ Above Average	❑ Average	❑ Below Average
Teamwork	Is this staff member helpful to co-workers, willing to change schedules, and cooperative with supervisors?	❑ Above Average	❑ Average	❑ Below Average
Leadership	Does this staff member have the courage of his/her convictions; stands up for and does what is right with tact and diplomacy?	❑ Above Average	❑ Average	❑ Below Average
Diversity	Are co-workers valued as team members and treated with respect, dignity, and professionalism by this staff member?	❑ Above Average	❑ Average	❑ Below Average
Quality	Does this staff member's work ethic create a positive example for others to emulate?	❑ Above Average	❑ Average	❑ Below Average
Compassion	Does this staff member show a sense of pride in how he/she applies him/herself to the job?	❑ Above Average	❑ Average	❑ Below Average

Comments: _____

_____

_____

_____

_____

_____

_____

_____

_____

_____

I. Exempt Employee Reviews

Some organizations provide a separate review form for exempt employees. The feedback differs from that given to nonexempt employees in that it is less focused on issues like attendance and production and more on results.

Employee Appraised: _____   Date: _____

Position: _____   Date Employed: _____

Location: _____   Department: _____

Exempt Salaried Performance Evaluation

Performance Evaluation Definitions

Outstanding

Substantially exceeds expectations; employee *consistently* exceeds *all* job requirements. Performance is recognized as clearly exceptional.

Commendable

Exceeds expectations; employee handles job assignments in a very able manner and frequently performs tasks beyond normal job requirements.

Meets Performance Expectations

Attains the high expectations of [Company]; employee is fully qualified, meets *all* performance expectations, and handles job assignments in a manner consistent with the high standards of [Company].

Marginal

Almost attains expectations; employee does not meet expectations on all job requirements but is judged capable of improvement and progression toward meeting performance expectations. A specific developmental plan must accompany this performance level.

Unsatisfactory

Falls substantially short of expectations; employee is not performing in an acceptable manner. Specific, written performance objectives must be prepared, and the employee's performance must be reviewed again in no more than six months.

1	2	3	4	5	6	7	8	9	10
Unsatisfactory		**Marginal**		**Meets Performance Expectations**		**Commendable**		**Outstanding**	

Occupational/Technical Knowledge   **Rating:**   ❏ ❏ ❏ ❏ ❏ ❏ ❏ ❏ ❏ ❏   **(Click on One)**
1 2 3 4 5 6 7 8 9 10

The area covers the employee's knowledge of his/her functions and responsibilities. It includes both knowledge that immediately impacts work functions and general knowledge of the field. Does the employee know how his/her function impacts other functions? The business? Is the incumbent considered an expert in his/her field or does he/she require a lot of help from others?

Planning   **Rating:**   ❏ ❏ ❏ ❏ ❏ ❏ ❏ ❏ ❏ ❏   **(Click on One)**
1 2 3 4 5 6 7 8 9 10

Does the employee realistically anticipate work and what resources will be needed to accomplish it? Is this done appropriately in advance? Does the employee make effective backup plans? Can the employee adapt to change, identify alternate action plans? Are they consistent with a customer focus?

Problem Solving   **Rating:**   ❏ ❏ ❏ ❏ ❏ ❏ ❏ ❏ ❏ ❏   **(Click on One)**
1 2 3 4 5 6 7 8 9 10

This area covers the employee's effectiveness at defining an issue, diagnosing a problem and analyzing causes, recommending and implementing solutions. Does the employee's cause analysis include reading materials, using outside sources or internal groups and/or individuals to increase understanding and to develop sound solutions? Is the employee an effective problem solver? Does he/she regularly exercise sound judgment?

Organizing   **Rating:**   ❏ ❏ ❏ ❏ ❏ ❏ ❏ ❏ ❏ ❏   **(Click on One)**
1 2 3 4 5 6 7 8 9 10

This area covers the determining, assembling, and arranging of resources (personnel, material, time, and facilities to accomplish objectives). Is the employee effective in establishing and, if needed, rethinking priorities?

Decision Making   Rating: ❑ ❑ ❑ ❑ ❑ ❑ ❑ ❑ ❑ ❑   (Click on One)
                                         1 2 3 4 5 6 7 8 9 10

Does the employee make decisions and recommendations or does he/she tend to shy away from making them? Does the employee attempt to get you or others to make his/her decisions? Does the employee make decisions without getting input from you or others who have a stake in the decision? Does the employee analyze and consider alternatives? Does the employee show originality in his/her decisions?

Self-Management Skills   Rating: ❑ ❑ ❑ ❑ ❑ ❑ ❑ ❑ ❑ ❑   (Click on One)
                                         1 2 3 4 5 6 7 8 9 10

Does the employee consistently demonstrate adaptability and flexibility in the job without losing effective control? Does the employee remain effective and display self-confidence in dealing with difficult situations and take corrective action, as required?

Results   Rating: ❑ ❑ ❑ ❑ ❑ ❑ ❑ ❑ ❑ ❑   (Click on One)
                                         1 2 3 4 5 6 7 8 9 10

This factor involves the execution of plans and programs to achieve desired results. The emphasis is on the ability to work effectively, both individually and in groups; the taking of responsibility and initiative; the handling of new situations; and the meeting of established deadlines and objectives.

Communicating   Rating: ❑ ❑ ❑ ❑ ❑ ❑ ❑ ❑ ❑ ❑   (Click on One)
                                         1 2 3 4 5 6 7 8 9 10

This factor deals with the skills of communicating effectively in the interest of good results. Does he/she keep supervisors, associates, and subordinates fully informed about work progress, problems, and with adequate feedback on the actual work? Does the employee communicate well orally? Is he/she effective in participating in groups? Does he/she listen well? Foster open communication? Does the individual communicate well in writing?

Interpersonal Skills and Relationships   Rating: ❑ ❑ ❑ ❑ ❑ ❑ ❑ ❑ ❑ ❑   (Click on One)
                                                       1 2 3 4 5 6 7 8 9 10

This factor refers to the ability of an individual to establish and maintain **effective** contacts within or outside the company in order to establish goodwill, conduct negotiations, render services, etc. Can the employee manage conflict? Does the employee value diverse work-styles, approaches, and thoughts? Does the employee treat others with respect and fairness? Cite specific instances of favorable or unfavorable relationships.

Leadership   Rating: ❑ ❑ ❑ ❑ ❑ ❑ ❑ ❑ ❑ ❑   (Click on One)
                                         1 2 3 4 5 6 7 8 9 10

This area covers the ability to reach goals through the effort of others. It is important to achieve results through the work of others that surround the individual in the organization, i.e., subordinates, associates, and superiors, through items such as: Does the employee encourage others to assume responsibility? What has the employee done to develop his/her subordinates? Does he/she promote/enforce safety and quality issues? Does the employee foster teamwork? Is he/she active in coaching and developing others?

Summary of Ratings

Summarize ratings previously given to provide a profile of the individual appraised.

Occupational/Technical Knowledge	
Planning	
Problem Solving	
Organizing	
Decision Making	
Self-Management Skills	
Results	
Communicating	
Interpersonal Skills and Relationships	
Leadership	
Overall Performance Rating	

Future Goals/Objectives To Be Achieved

1. Specific plans for continuing performance in present position. Attach additional description/narrative if warranted (indicate performance objectives, activity required, and target dates):

    _____

    _____

    _____

    _____

    _____

    _____

    _____

    _____

2. Specific plans for continuing personal development. Attach additional description/narrative if warranted (indicate personal improvement objectives, activities required, and target dates).

    _____

    _____

    _____

    _____

    _____

    _____

    _____

    _____

3. Supervisor's general comments:

    _____

    _____

    _____

    _____

    _____

    _____

    _____

    _____

Prepared by: _____   _____
                          (supervisor)   (date prepared)

Reviewed by: _____   _____
                                                                    (date reviewed)

I have received this performance evaluation and agree with it except as noted:

Signed by: _____   _____
                          (employee)   (date discussed)

Salaried Employee Performance Appraisal

(With Addendum for Supervisory Personnel)

Employee Information

Employee Name:_____   **Date of Appraisal:** _____ / _____ / _____

Position: _____   **Location:**_____

Reason for Appraisal: **Introductory**   **6-month**   **12-month**   **Annual**   **Other:** _____
(Circle Only One)

Appraisal Period - From: _____ / _____   **To:**   _____ / _____

Supervisor Information

Appraising Supervisor: _____   **Title:** _____

Appraisal Objective: The objective of the performance appraisal is to facilitate open and honest communication between an employee and his/her supervisor regarding their work performance. This is accomplished by:

1. Gaining feedback from employees on how they feel about their job performance,
2. Informing employees on how their supervisor sees their performance as compared with established work standards,
3. Providing an opportunity to discuss and agree upon ways in which acceptable performance can be maintained and poor performance corrected.

Appraised Employee: Please read the appraisal thoroughly and discuss the contents of the appraisal with your appraising supervisor. You are encouraged to write your comments in the space provided and openly discuss each item prior to signing the appraisal. Please remember that the objective of this appraisal is to provide you a better understanding of how your job performance is perceived by your supervisor in relation to established job standards and to provide you an opportunity to discuss your performance. You are encouraged to take full advantage of this opportunity to openly discuss your performance with your supervisor.

Performance Ratings Guide

5 = Distinguished   Conspicuously meritorious performance. Consistently exceeds all job requirements.

4 = Excellent   Generally exceeds requirements with minimum guidance. Above average performance.

3 = Satisfactory   Job requirements met in a wholly satisfactory manner. Some supervision or guidance needed.

2 = Marginal   Improvement needed in key job requirements. Considerable supervision or guidance required.

1 = Unsatisfactory   Major shortcoming in meeting job requirements. Requires corrective action or separation is eminent if performance improvement is unsuccessful. Continuous guidance required.

Performance Factors/Criteria	Performance Rating
	circle one

1. Adherence to Company Policy: 1   2   3   4   5
- Follows guidelines as established by policies
- Conforms to Company and job standards and requirements, shows respect for others
- Acts in the best interests of the Company at all times, serves as an example for others
- Conducts business in an ethical fashion

Comments - Employee and Supervisor *(Use back of sheet if more room is needed)* _____

_____

_____

2. Job Knowledge: 1   2   3   4   5
- Demonstrates a thorough understanding of his/her job processes and procedures
- Integrates knowledge to efficiently accomplish job requirements
- Efficiently uses resources (including management) to obtain additional knowledge

Comments - Employee and Supervisor *(Use back of sheet if more room is needed)* _____

_____

_____

3. Cooperativeness: 1   2   3   4   5
- Consistently supports management decisions as demonstrated by his/her actions
- Demonstrates a "can do" attitude by responding positively to instructions
- Follows instructions and works harmoniously with others to complete the job or task

Comments - Employee and Supervisor *(Use back of sheet if more room is needed)* _____

_____

_____

4. Commitment: 1   2   3   4   5
- Extent that employee is committed to their job and to the success of the Company
- Continuously puts forth the effort to achieve goals and continuous quality improvement
- Degree to which employee goes the extra step to ensure job/task completion

Comments - Employee and Supervisor *(Use back of sheet if more room is needed)* _____

_____

_____

5. Safety: 1   2   3   4   5
- Degree to which employee is committed to providing and maintaining a safe work place
- Reports all unsafe working conditions to supervisor or management team
- Corrects unsafe work conditions as directed
- Follows all safety polices such as: [List of Policies]

Comments - Employee and Supervisor *(Use back of sheet if more room is needed)* _____

_____

_____

Total Performance Score From Page 1: _____

Performance Factors/Criteria	Performance Rating
	circle one

6. Quantity of Work (Productivity):   1   2   3   4   5
- High volume producer, always puts forth the effort to maximize productivity
- Meets or exceeds established work deadlines
- Engages him- her-self in a productive work effort whenever possible
- Meets production goals and objectives

Comments - Employee and Supervisor *(Use back of sheet if more room is needed)* _____

_____

_____

7. Quality of Work: 1   2   3   4   5
- Produces work that is accurate and reliable
- Work is accomplished quickly and efficiently
- Works in a thorough and organized manner while minimizing down time
- Results are consistently within acceptable quality standards

Comments - Employee and Supervisor *(Use back of sheet if more room is needed)* _____

_____

_____

8. Reliability: 1   2   3   4   5
- Completes responsibilities with minimal direct supervision
- Follows through with assigned jobs and tasks all the way through completion
- Puts forth the effort to achieve goals and objectives under varying circumstances

Comments - Employee and Supervisor *(Use back of sheet if more room is needed)* _____

_____

_____

9. Attendance: 1   2   3   4   5
- Meets or exceeds punctuality and attendance expectations/requirements
- Faithfully reports to work and conforms to scheduled work hours
- When necessitated, follows call-in procedures and informs others of absences

Comments - Employee and Supervisor *(Use back of sheet if more room is needed)* _____

_____

_____

10. Communication: 1   2   3   4   5
- Exhibits good interpersonal skills
- Develops and fosters professional relationships with co-workers and vendors
- Keeps others informed as dictated by operational demands and need-to-know
- Keeps self informed of announcements made via established Company venues

Comments - Employee and Supervisor *(Use back of sheet if more room is needed)* _____

_____

_____

Total Performance Score From Page 2: _____

*** This Section for Supervisory Personnel Only ***

Performance Factors/Criteria	Performance Rating
	circle one

11. Leadership: 1 2 3 4 5
- Trains, develops, and motivates subordinates to contribute toward department goals
- Selects, directs, and coordinates activities of others to meet performance requirements
- Leads by example and serves as a role model
- Follows through with directives and tasks

Comments - Employee and Supervisor *(Use back of sheet if more room is needed)* _____

_____

_____

12. Controlling and Directing: 1 2 3 4 5
- Degree to which supervisor monitors and enforces Company policies on others
- Holds others responsible for their actions, to include safety and housekeeping procedures
- Delegates authority while accepting responsibility for his/her actions
- Counsels and directs improvement as needed

Comments - Employee and Supervisor *(Use back of sheet if more room is needed)* _____

_____

_____

13. Planning and Organizing: 1 2 3 4 5
- Analyzes work load, establishes realistic work and production goals, meets deadlines
- Demonstrates effective time management with self and that of subordinates
- Anticipates business needs, plans ahead, effectively organizes work and personnel

Comments - Employee and Supervisor *(Use back of sheet if more room is needed)* _____

_____

_____

14. Decision Making: 1 2 3 4 5
- Ability to make decisions in a timely fashion
- Makes quality decisions after considering all applicable information and processes
- Demonstrates problem-solving capabilities
- Shows a sense of initiative by anticipating operational needs and preparing accordingly

Comments - Employee and Supervisor *(Use back of sheet if more room is needed)* _____

_____

_____

15. Operational Results/Goals (As Specified): 1 2 3 4 5

Comments - Employee and Supervisor *(Use back of sheet if more room is needed)* _____

_____

_____

Total Performance Score From Page 3: _____

★★★ All Salaried Personnel Complete This Section ★★★

Employee Name: _____   **Department:** _____

Job Title: _____   **Appraisal Period:** _____

Strengths: Please list your top three strengths and how you applied them to your position.

1. _____
_____
_____

2. _____
_____
_____

3. _____
_____
_____

Accomplishments: Please list your top three accomplishments during this evaluation period.

1. _____
_____
_____

2. _____
_____
_____

3. _____
_____
_____

Appraising Supervisor Complete This Form

Employee Appraised: _____   **Department:** _____

Job Title:_____   **Appraisal Period:** _____

Goals and Objectives: Please list the top objectives or areas of improvement for the appraised employee.

1. _____

   _____

   _____

2. _____

   _____

   _____

3. _____

   _____

   _____

4. _____

   _____

   _____

Total Performance Score from Pages 1 and 2 (and Page 3 if Applicable): _____

I acknowledge receipt and understanding of the above employee appraisal.

Employee Signature: _____   **Date :** _____ / _____ / _____

Supervisor Signature: _____   **Date :** _____ / _____ / _____

HR Manager Signature:_____   **Date :** _____ / _____ / _____

Exempt Employee Performance Evaluation

The purpose of this performance evaluation is to serve as a format for discussing the employee's past performance, the strengths and areas for improvement, in order to assist the employee in improving his/her performance. This is also a tool for the employee to inform the supervisor of his/her needs for personal development.

Section I - Review employee's performance. Consider time on this job when assessing the employee's performance.

Note that there are four levels in which to rate performance.

Definition of Performance Levels

Above Expectations: Performance is consistently and significantly above job expectations and requirements. Demonstrates the willingness to assume additional responsibilities.

Meets Expectations: Performance regularly accomplishes what is expected. Performance demonstrates the required skills and knowledge for the position and sometimes exceeds expectations

Below Expectations: Performance meets only the minimum requirements, which could be improved through development, experience, and/or application. Performance is below accepted levels for the time in the position.

Unacceptable: Performance is clearly below acceptable levels. Has not kept pace with expectations, successes have only been occasional, or performance has been deteriorating. Immediate corrective action is required.

Use the comment space in each area to write *specific examples* supporting each rating. Below is a list of ideas and questions for each category you may want to consider when writing comments.

Effectiveness - Plans work duties, activities, and programs for an efficient and coordinated workflow to achieve desired objectives. Does the person develop and analyze courses of action, as well as select, recommend, and implement the best option? Does the employee gather relevant information and gather sufficient quantity and quality of data? Does he/she personally or jointly establish specific goals and objectives? Does the person plan the appropriate assignment of personnel and allocations of resources? Does the employee differentiate between the important and unimportant actions in establishing priorities?

Leadership - Does the employee delegate according to the individual's skill, knowledge, abilities, and attitude? Does the person inspire and guide individuals toward goal achievement? Does the employee establish and completely communicate a clear vision of the desired future state? Does the employee foster the attitudes, conditions, and environments that yield improved quality and quantity of individual and team performance? Does the employee develop and build upon the suggestions and ideas offered?

Initiative - Does the employee generate and develop new ideas to improve existing and future conditions and results? Does the employee recognize possible and probable courses of action? Does he/she consider the pros and cons of each course of action? Does the person make effective and efficient decisions that improve situations? Does the employee make efficient use of time in carrying out responsibilities and day-to-day actions?

Knowledge of Work - Does the employee have sufficient training and experience to adequately do the job? Does the employee need more on the job training? Should the employee be cross-trained in other areas? Is supplemental training such as writing skills, basic speech, ESL, etc., required? Is performance on the job consistent with training and background? What facet of the job does the employee do best? How can we help to build on strengths and improve areas needing improvement?

Teamwork/Communication - Is this person flexible and willing to try different approaches to problems/people? Does the person demonstrate a desire to look for different ways to deal with people/problems if an initial approach does not succeed? Will the person support a group decision even if the person has a dissenting point of view? Does the person identify problems that he/she can control/influence?

Organizational Participation - Describe any organizational participation in which the employee has engaged during the period covered by this review. Has the employee participated in the [Company Program]? Has the employee participated in in-house committees?

Section II - Summary of Performance. In this section assess the employee's total performance. Highlight exceptional items and areas for improvement/training needs. Outline expectations for the coming year and comment on what additional training and/or experience the employee needs to enhance his/her effectiveness. Below are the three areas in which to summarize the individual's performance.

Stop - these things that are hindering your effectiveness and performance.

Start - focusing on these expectations that will help to improve your effectiveness and performance.

Continue - to exhibit these strengths that are encouraged and appreciated.

Section III - Employee Comments. All employees are encouraged to comment on their evaluation. Please allow sufficient time for this process.

Section IV - Discussion of review with employee and signatures.

Section V - Fiscal Year Business Plan.   Following the formal performance appraisal, discuss and establish expectations for the employee that support the department's/plant's business plan for the ensuing fiscal year. Expectations for specific initiatives, customer satisfaction, teamwork, and communications; and personal development should be identified and target dates established for attainment or completion.

To ensure this process works well, both the employee and evaluating supervisor are encouraged to openly discuss the expectations in all aspects of this process. The evaluating supervisor is expected to actively seek feedback from the employee; the employee should freely exchange ideas with the supervisor. The overall goal of both participants should be to achieve consensus on the expectations.

A performance progress review is required for each employee. This will be an informal review using the Performance Progress Review form as a tool to discuss problems or any areas that need development. During this review, revisit this section and check on the status of the employee's business plan. The supervisor will retain the progress review forms to aid in completion of the annual Performance Evaluation, and a copy will be forwarded to Human Resources. If the employee transfers to another department or plant during the year, the progress review forms will be transferred to the new supervisor.

Then, prior to the next annual performance evaluation, discuss the status of the initiatives and use this as a stepping stone for the next year's business plan.

Exempt Employee Performance Evaluation

Employee Name (First, Middle, Last) _____ Department and Job Title _____

Review Period: ❏ 90-Day Evaluation   ❏ Annual Evaluation   ❏ Other _____

Employment Date _____ Full-Hire Date _____ Review Date _____

Definition of Performance Levels

Above Expectations: Performance is consistently and significantly above job expectations and requirements. Demonstrates the willingness to assume additional responsibilities.

Meets Expectations: Performance regularly accomplishes what is expected. Performance demonstrates the required skills and knowledge for the position and sometimes exceeds expectations.

Below Expectations: Performance meets only the minimum requirements, which could be improved through development, experience, and/or application. Performance is below accepted levels for the time in the position.

Unacceptable: Performance is clearly below acceptable levels. Has not kept pace with expectations, successes have only been occasional, or performance has been deteriorating. Immediate corrective action is required.

Section I   Review employee's performance by checking the most appropriate block in each category based on time on the job. Write specific examples supporting each rating.

Effectiveness - Carries out work assignments and tasks while meeting time, budget, and quality commitments with little or no supervision. Completes high-quality work according to plans. Has the ability to improve procedures and processes.

❏ **Above Expectations**   ❏ **Meets Expectations**   ❏ **Below Expectations**   ❏ **Unacceptable**

Comments: _____

_____

_____

_____

_____

_____

Leadership - Gains support and cooperation of work group and others. Utilizes employees' abilities effectively to achieve results.

❏ **Above Expectations**   ❏ **Meets Expectations**   ❏ **Below Expectations**   ❏ **Unacceptable**

Comments: _____

_____

_____

_____

_____

_____

Initiative - Willingness to make significant contributions with little direction, voluntarily starts projects, attempts non-routine jobs and tasks. The degree to which the employee is self-starting and proactive.

❏ **Above Expectations**   ❏ **Meets Expectations**   ❏ **Below Expectations**   ❏ **Unacceptable**

Comments: _____

_____

_____

_____

_____

Knowledge of Work - Learns and applies acquired skills and technical and professional knowledge to the job requirements.

❑ **Above Expectations**　　❑ **Meets Expectations**　　❑ **Below Expectations**　　❑ **Unacceptable**

Comments: _____

_____

_____

_____

_____

Teamwork/Communication - Facilitates a positive and productive team-oriented work environment and encourages open communications throughout the organization.

❑ **Above Expectations**　　❑ **Meets Expectations**　　❑ **Below Expectations**　　❑ **Unacceptable**

Comments: _____

_____

_____

_____

_____

Organizational Participation - Describe any organizational participation in which the employee has engaged during the period covered by this review.

❑ **Above Expectations**　　❑ **Meets Expectations**　　❑ **Below Expectations**　　❑ **Unacceptable**

[Program]	**[Program]**	**[Program]**	**[Program]**	**Other:** ❑
❑ Yes ❑ No ❑ Trained	❑ Yes ❑ No ❑ Trained	❑ Yes ❑ No ❑ Trained	❑ Yes ❑ No ❑ Trained	_____
If yes how many? _____	If yes how many? _____	If yes how many? _____	If yes how many? _____	Please explain.

Comments: _____

_____

_____

_____

_____

Section II　　Summary of Performance - Supervisor's Appraisal

Stop - these things that are hindering your effectiveness and performance.

_____

_____

_____

Start - focusing on these expectations that will help to improve your effectiveness and performance.

_____

_____

_____

Continue - to exhibit these strengths that are encouraged and appreciated.

_____

_____

_____

Section III   Employee Comments: Each individual evaluated is encouraged to add any comments to this review.

_____

_____

_____

_____

_____

_____

_____

Section IV   Discussion of Review With Employee and Signatures - The contents of this form have been reviewed with me:

Employee Signature _____   Date _____

Evaluating Supervisor _____   Date _____

Department Manager _____   Date _____

Human Resources _____   Date _____

Section V   Fiscal Year Business Plan

Business Plan - *Specific Initiatives*	Activity Plan				Status As Of				Countermeasures
	Q1	Q2	Q3	Q4	Q1	Q2	Q3	Q4	
Customer Satisfaction									
Teamwork and Communication									
Personal Development									

☿-Indicator   ☐-Completed   ●-On Track   △ - Slippage, Will Recover   X- Will Not Meet Target

Team Member Signature _____   Date _____

Leader Signature _____   Date _____

J. Job-Specific Reviews

In organizations where a large number of people perform the same job, it may be appropriate to develop a review form around the specific duties for the classification.

1. **Performance Evaluation and Development Plan— Fulfillment Department:** Focuses on performance in relation to established performance objectives, page 195

2. **Weighted Performance Evaluation for Construction Field Employees:** Uses job traits as performance factors but provides evaluation check-boxes that are job-specific and ranked, page 199

3. **Annual Evaluation: Job Coach/Supported Employment Program:** Lists and weights specific job duties and provides space for narrative feedback, page 203

4. **Performance Evaluation—Job-Specific Related Skills Administrative Tech II:** Summarizes specific job duties and provides behavioral-based ratings, page 205

Performance Evaluation and Development Plan—Fulfillment Department

High performance standards, candid feedback, clear goals/accountability, and an intense focus on "what we need to do better" do not guarantee success, but without them we cannot hope to build the world's most customer-centric company.

Employee Info

Employee Name: _____

Employee Position:_____

Department: _____

Reviewer Info

Reviewer Name: _____

Reviewer Position: _____

Review Date: _____

Rating	Definition of Rating
5.0	Exceptional performance, rarely achieved. Achieves results well beyond the scope of the position. Demonstrates the highest standards of performance relative to peers.
4.5	Consistently exceeds all position requirements and expectations. Accomplishments are highly valued and often are beyond the scope of the position. Demonstrates higher standards of performance relative to peers.
4.0	Consistently exceeds most position requirements and expectations. Accomplishments are often noteworthy. Overall performance is consistently above the quality and quantity of peers.
3.5	Exceeds some position requirements and expectations. Successfully accomplishes all objectives. Overall performance consistently matches the quality and quantity of peers.
3.0	Meets position requirements and expectations. Accomplishes most or all objectives. Some aspects of overall performance may require additional development or improvement to match the quality and quantity of peers.
2.5	Falls below some performance standards and expectations of the job. Demonstrates one or more performance deficiencies that hinder acceptable performance. Some aspects of overall performance will require additional development or improvement to match the quality and quantity of peers.
1.0–2.0	Does not meet minimum requirements in critical aspects of the job and has numerous performance deficiencies that prevent success at [Company].

Competencies

Customer Focus   Rating: _____

Demonstrates accuracy in work performance, pays attention to detail. Has a passion for meeting customer needs and providing mistake-free service.

_____

_____

_____

Ownership   Rating: _____

Takes ownership of completed work and work area in general. Takes pride in [Company].

_____

_____

_____

Achieves the Right Results

Rating: _____

Works at steady and productive pace without distraction. Remains focused throughout the shift. Is aware of and works toward department goals.

_____

_____

_____

Teamwork

Rating: _____

Values and contributes with a positive attitude to our collective goals and daily responsibilities. Communicates effectively with managers and other employees. Treats all with respect and helps foster good group morale.

_____

_____

_____

Job Knowledge

Rating: _____

Has learned job responsibilities quickly and applies knowledge accurately. Knows the appropriate methods of operation in the department.

_____

_____

_____

Leadership

Rating: _____

Exhibits leadership qualities, can lead by example. Shares information that helps others do their job well.

_____

_____

_____

Dependability

Rating: _____

Demonstrates reliability and responsibility by following a job through to completion. Adheres to work schedule and attendance policy.

_____

_____

_____

Initiative

Rating: _____

Seeks opportunities to learn new tasks and accepts new responsibilities.

_____

_____

_____

Flexibility   **Rating:** _____

Responds well to changes in workplace (i.e., job functions, work schedules, etc.). Able to adapt quickly to evolving priorities. Open to ideas for improvement.

_____

_____

_____

Problem Solving   **Rating:** _____

Able to identify problems and resources for resolution. Able to investigate and help take action to meet customer needs.

_____

_____

_____

Safety   **Rating:** _____

Performs job safely. Understands and adheres to general safety rules. Able to identify safety hazards and notify management.

_____

_____

_____

Summary/Overall Potential   **Rating:** _____

Rating of overall performance.

_____

_____

_____

Goal Development

List goals to be achieved, and by what date:

_____

_____

_____

_____

_____

_____

_____

_____

_____

_____

_____

Comments

Employee Comments: *Comments can address work assignment, the review process, or the company as a whole.*

_____

_____

_____

_____

_____

_____

_____

_____

Employee's Signature _____ Date _____

Your signature does not necessarily mean you agree, but affirms this review has been discussed in detail between you and your reviewer.

Reviewer's Signature _____ Date _____

Operations Manager _____

Senior Operations Manager _____

Wage Increase Amount _____ **Next Review Date** _____

Approved by Operations Manager _____ Date _____

Weighted Performance Evaluation
for Construction Field Employees

Employee Name: _____

Date of Last Review: _____

Hire Date: _____

Current Pay: _____

Pay Changed to: _____

Reason for Report: ❑ 90-Day   ❑ Annual   ❑ Promotion   ❑ Other _____

Supervisor: _____

Current Position: _____

Current Pay Range: _____

Period Covered By This Report: From _____ To_____

Effective Date:_____

Performance Factors	Performance Measures

Dependability: amount of supervision required for employee to get job done

Comments: _____

_____

_____

15   ❑ Self-starter – rarely needs direct supervision.

12   ❑ Needs some supervision, but usually dependable on routine work.

10   ❑ Conscientious, but requires occasional supervision.

5   ❑ Needs frequent supervision and reorientation on job responsibilities.

3   ❑ Needs constant supervision to get job done.

Safety: willingness to follow safety requirements.

Comments: _____

_____

_____

15   ❑ Very safety-conscious. Understands and always follows good safety practices.

12   ❑ Good understanding of safety. Rarely fails to follow procedures.

10   ❑ Typical worker in job. Generally follows procedures. Occasionally makes safety mistakes.

5   ❑ Needs help in safe work practices. Sometimes fails to use proper equipment or follow procedures.

0   ❑ Does not follow safety practices. Warnings issued for violation of safety rules.

Attendance: complies with company standards in absence; shows up on time.

Comments: _____

_____

_____

15   ❑ Outstanding record of attendance and punctuality.

12   ❑ Rarely absent or late.

10   ❑ Occasionally absent or late. Always notifies in advance.

5   ❑ Some problems with attendance, punctuality, or misuse of time.

0   ❑ Has serious problems with attendance.

Employee was _____ times late in the last _____ months.

Employee was _____ times absent in the last _____ months.

Cooperation: willingness to accept supervision, ability to get along with co-workers; team player.

Comments: _____

_____

_____

15   ❑ Responds with enthusiasm to job assignments; always willing to do whatever is necessary to get the job done.

10   ❑ Usually responds well to supervision and co-workers.

8   ❑ Gets along well with supervisors and co-workers.

3   ❑ Needs prompting, little initiative, or occasional conflicts with supervisor or co-workers.

0   ❑ Resents directions, resists working with others, frequent conflicts.

Job knowledge: amount of skill in performing job; understanding of job procedures and equipment. Comments: _____ _____ _____	20 15 10 5 0	❏ Has completely mastered all phases of job. Uses equipment with great skill; is able to help others. ❏ Thorough knowledge of most job requirements. Competent with equipment. ❏ Typical knowledge and skills. Sometimes needs assistance or direction. ❏ Insufficient knowledge or skill to perform job unassisted. Requires frequent instruction on equipment. ❏ Relies on others constantly; does not know procedures or use of equipment.
Adaptability: ability to learn quickly; ability and willingness to adjust to changes in job assignments, personnel, or surroundings. Comments: _____ _____ _____	15 12 9 0	❏ Quick to catch on. Welcomes new assignments. Undisturbed by changes. ❏ Learns well and willingly. Accepts change. ❏ Average learner. Adjusts to changes with minimum difficulty. ❏ Does not remember assignments. Resists change.
Quantity of Work: ability to meet or exceed expected goals; use of time and willingness to "keep at it." Comments: _____ _____ _____	20 15 10 5 0	❏ Always puts in "full day's work." Works quickly and productively. ❏ Diligent worker. Regularly meets expectations. Makes good use of time. ❏ Usually completes work assignments within time allowed. ❏ Sometimes gets behind, not very effective use of time. Work speed lower than average. ❏ Has trouble meeting job assignments. Work speed poor. Requires help or constant supervision to complete assignments.
Quality of work: ability to meet expected standards; "getting it right the first time"; avoiding errors. Comments: _____ _____ _____	25 20 15 8 0	❏ Very high quality of work. Follows required procedures exactly. Rarely makes mistakes or has to do work over. ❏ Overall quality of work is very good. Occasional mistakes, but self-corrected. ❏ Quality is typical. ❏ Needs some improvement in quality of work. Fails to follow procedures; frequent mistakes. ❏ Quality of work does not meet standards.
Heavy Equipment: (if applicable) ability to use and care for equipment. Comments: _____ _____ _____	20 15 8 0 10	❏ Highly skilled operator; excellent respect for equipment. ❏ Competent operator, usually takes appropriate care of equipment. ❏ Occasionally careless, has possibly caused some minor damage. ❏ Does not follow equipment operation rules or disregards safety requirements. ❏ Is not assigned to operate equipment.

Small Tools: ability to use and care for company tools.

Comments: _____

_____

_____

15 ❏ Careful with tools; uses them appropriately and skillfully.

10 ❏ Typical employee, usually takes reasonable care of equipment.

5 ❏ Occasionally careless, has possibly caused some minor damage or failed to return tools.

0 ❏ Abuses tools or does not follow safety and use precautions.

Appearance: as relates to job.

Comments: _____

_____

_____

10 ❏ Always appropriately dressed, including use of safety equipment.

5 ❏ Typical in dress for job.

0 ❏ Requires frequent reminders to follow dress requirements.

Total Score: add values of all ratings checked.

❏ 160–185 Exceptional

❏ 125–159 Very Good

❏ 85–124 Typical

❏ Below 85 Needs Improvement

Additional comments by supervisor:

What are employee's strengths related to his/her *present* position? _____

_____

What are the employee's weaknesses related to his/her *present* position? _____

_____

What specific instruction, training, or experience do you recommend for this employee in the coming year? _____

_____

What, in your opinion, is the best next job assignment or promotion for this employee? _____

What additional training or experience would be necessary for him/her to qualify for that position? _____

_____

Employee Comments:

_____

_____

_____

_____

Employee: I have read this evaluation and it has been explained to me. My signature below does not necessarily indicate agreement with the evaluation, and I have had the opportunity to express my opinion and to discuss my performance with my Supervisor.

Employee Signature _____ Date _____

Supervisor Signature _____ Date _____

Area Supt. Signature _____ Date _____

Officer Signature _____ Date _____

Annual Evaluation:
Job Coach/Supported Employment Program

Employee: _____   Date of Review: _____

Appraisal Period: _____   Reviewer: _____

Rating Table	
1. ABR: Above and beyond requirements	104–113
2. EMR: Exceeds most job requirements	114–245
3. MR: Meets job requirements	246–377
4. MSR: Meets some requirements	378–510
5. FMR: Fails to meet job requirements	511–520

Duties/Responsibilities	Weight	Evaluation	Criteria	Comments
		Rating	Commendations/Discipline	Documentation
Contribute to development and implementation of [Plan] on assigned participants.	10			
Participate in scheduled staffings and contribute to the evaluation of participant's performance and revisions of the [Plan].	10			
Work directly with participants to ensure that goals and objectives, procedures, time frames, and responsibilities assigned involve active participation of individuals.	15			
Work directly with employers to gain knowledge of goals developed from employer performance evaluations. Gain active support and participation of employers, co-workers, etc., as appropriate and agreed to by the participant.	5			
Train, evaluate, and monitor all participants in their work skills and social behaviors.	5			
Provide transportation or transportation training to job sites as required by the [Plan].	3			
Schedule ancillary services for participants as required to maintain the job, while covering gaps in recreational, social, medical, and psychological services not addressed on the worksite.	2			
Provide training and support to employers, co-workers, and worker's support group identified in the [Plan] to facilitate participant's inclusion in the workforce and quality of life.	15			

Duties/Responsibilities	Weight	Evaluation	Criteria	Comments
		Rating	Commendations/Discipline	Documentation
Participate in off-site meetings and training opportunities by the [Company] or off-site providers.	5			
Maintain accurate participant performance records. Complete all records, reports, and forms required by funding agencies and policies and procedures, per established schedule.	10			
Additional Items Attend meetings/training	1			
Work Habits Attendance	20			
Communication of problems	1			
Takes direction	1			
Solicits advice	1			
Cumulative Rating				

Current Wage/Salary: _____

Areas To Be Improved/Goals With Time Frame:

   1. _____

   2. _____

   3. _____

Reviewer Comments:

_____

_____

_____

_____

Employee Comments:

_____

_____

_____

_____

Employee Signature _____ Date _____

Supervisor Signature _____ Date _____

Performance Evaluation—Job-Specific Related Skills

Administrative Tech II

Employee Name: _____   Position: _____

Supervisor: _____   Department: _____

Date of Evaluation: _____   Evaluation Period From: _____ To _____

1. Customer Support: Maintains courtesy and diplomacy with customers, and/or job contractors and to other external contacts as well as internal contacts; makes self available to respond to customer needs; prevents unnecessary delays for customers; communicates appropriate information to the customer effectively and accurately; listens effectively.

Sup Emp

❑ ❑   1 Fails to interact appropriately with customers. Often discourteous and unwilling to help.

❑ ❑   2 Seldom interacts appropriately with customers. Usually discourteous and unwilling to help.

❑ ❑   3 Regularly interacts appropriately with customers. Usually courteous and willing to help.

❑ ❑   4 Always interacts appropriately with customers. Always courteous and willing to help.

❑ ❑   5 Excellent interaction with customers. Efficient and effective with customer support. Provides customer support beyond supervisor's expectations.

Comments: _____

_____

2. Department Interaction: The ability to understand that your actions have an effect on the Department; work habits affecting the morale and job satisfaction with the Department; willingness to cooperate and be respectful of others level of skills and abilities; demonstrates flexibility; offers assistance and acknowledges others' work needs.

Sup Emp

❑ ❑   1 Fails to understand affect of behavior on Department's other members.

❑ ❑   2 Seldom tries to understand affect of behavior on Department's other members.

❑ ❑   3 Understands and regularly applies Department interaction.

❑ ❑   4 Always applies skills in Department interaction

❑ ❑   5 Has excellent skills in Department interaction.

Comments: _____

_____

3. Record Keeping: Ability of employee to originate clear and concise oral and written communication; to update information and provide accurate documentation in a timely manner; to understand the record keeping application and use it in an efficient manner to provide Departmental work-flow.

Sup Emp

❑ ❑   1 Fails to meet record keeping skills.

❑ ❑   2 Seldom meets record keeping skills.

❑ ❑   3 Regularly meets record keeping skills

❑ ❑   4 Always meets record keeping skills.

❑ ❑   5 Exceeds record keeping skills.

Comments: _____

_____

K. Other Forms and Tools

1. **Performance Management Process:** Defines performance traits for employee effectiveness, page 209

2. **Quarterly One-on-One Meeting with (manager's name):** Outlines and summarizes manager-employee meetings, page 211

3. **Performance Planning:** Provides a summary of goals and measures for employee performance, page 213

4. **Performance Review Planning Guide:** Tool for outlining review content to direct employee to continue current performance, improve poor performance, and accept new assignments or procedures, page 215

Performance Management Process

Key Success Factors Definitions

Listed below are the definitions of the key success factors that can be used in assessing an employee's effectiveness in relationship to a particular factor. Keep in mind that these definitions are not intended to be all-inclusive.

Proficiency in Job

- Applies the necessary knowledge and skills to the position's responsibilities.
- Considers the interrelationship between own job and other functions and applies the Company's policies and procedures.
- Results reflect accuracy, neatness, thoroughness, and professionalism.
- Establishes priorities and accomplishes the necessary steps to achieve objectives.

Communicating Information and Ideas

- Effectively and clearly exchanges information and ideas, both orally and in writing.
- Listens attentively.
- Conveys pertinent information regarding decisions or work changes to others in a timely manner.
- Facilitates and provides opportunities for feedback.
- Responds to phone calls quickly and handles complaints professionally.

Decision Making and Taking Action

- Assembles and evaluates relevant information and reaches sound conclusions.
- Makes appropriate recommendations, develops alternatives, or takes necessary actions within a reasonable time frame.
- Implements solutions consistent with the Company's values, goals, and strategies.
- Prevents difficult situations from accelerating and/or reoccurring.

Initiative and Resourcefulness

- Assumes ownership and completes work with minimal supervision and without prompting.
- Takes new and different approaches to familiar situations.
- Anticipates and prepares for potential problems or opportunities.
- Uses creativity to achieve results.

Managing Time

- Utilizes time effectively for maximum performance.
- Completes projects and tasks well within deadlines.
- Achieves desired results by establishing effective work priorities and methods.
- Dependable and reliable (consider absence and tardiness history).

Building Relationships

- Works effectively with others and responds positively to situations that require cooperation, courtesy, and tact.
- Provides customer (internal and external) service, which is responsive, courteous, and timely during routine and non-routine customer interactions.
- Encourages and assists others through training.
- Places the team's goals and objectives above individual goals and objectives.
- Demonstrates support for Company's products, policies, and philosophies.

Organizational and Administrative Effectiveness

- Operates efficiently at the lowest cost using good business judgment.
- Reduces waste and promotes an awareness of cost-saving measures.
- Effectively sets objectives, establishes time schedules, delegates responsibility, and responds to priorities to maximize impact and results.

Managing Conflict; Negotiating

- Resolves conflict effectively while practicing tact, flexibility, and open-mindedness.
- Demonstrates knowledge of issues and other parties' positions.
- Anticipates others' strategies.
- Displays influencing and persuasive ability.

Adaptability

- Willing and able to learn new processes, assignments, and/or challenges.
- Adjusts to changes in work, conditions, or unusual situations quickly.
- Accepts construction criticism, guidance, and special assignments.
- Adapts new knowledge or past experiences to various situations.
- Sets priorities while retaining flexibility and performs multiple tasks at a given time.

Energy and Drive

- Responds to requests for extra effort to deal with emergencies and heavy workloads.
- Works persistently despite constraints to accomplish objectives.

Integrity

- Promotes trust and respect.
- Acts reputably and honestly in relationships with others.
- Places the goals of the team before individual goals.

Self-Management and Development

- Accepts responsibility for own job, career growth, and development.
- Seeks out new or additional assignments.
- Assists in establishing accurate and reasonable goals that support Company objectives.
- Monitors performance towards goals and makes adjustments to facilitate goal achievement.
- Acts with self-discipline and in a professional manner.

Leadership

- Leads by example in a manner that positively contributes to the Company.
- Functions as a mentor for other employees.
- Motivates, stimulates, and positively influences others toward the attainment of common goals.

Safety

- Keeps the workplace safe, clean, uncluttered, and free of hazards.
- Uses and maintains equipment properly and safely.
- Observes safety regulations and remains alert to potential hazards when working or driving.

Selecting and Developing People

- Maintains appropriate staffing levels to ensure optimum productivity.
- Establishes and maintains standards of performance.
- Defines and delegates responsibilities and establishes goals in a clear and timely manner.
- Fosters individual growth, monitors performance, and provides constructive feedback through training, counseling, coaching, and appraisal.
- Identifies and addresses training needs.

Quarterly One-on-One Meeting with (manager's name)

Employee Name: _____

Date: _____

(Critical Items)   (Late Items)

Item Project, Issues, etc.	Date Started	Estimated Date of Completion	Assistance Needed; Issues to Resolve, etc.
1. Current Items:			
A.			
B.			
C.			
D.			
E.			
F.			
G.			
H.			
2. Items Completed:			
A.			
B.			
C.			

3. Areas where I can help you improve your skill set or improve your job performance:

A. _____

B. _____

C. _____

4. Personal Business Growth items completed last month, and future plans for Personal Business Growth:

A. _____

B. _____

C. _____

Performance Planning

Employee Name: _____   Performance Period: _____

Goals	Measures	Results Achieved

Performance Review Planning Guide

Essential functions: Most employees perform a variety of duties. An effective review discusses the most important assignments or responsibilities. Typically, these can be grouped into five or six major categories.

Goals

1. _____   ❑ Continue   ❑ Improve   ❑ New

   _____

2. _____   ❑ Continue   ❑ Improve   ❑ New

   _____

3. _____   ❑ Continue   ❑ Improve   ❑ New

   _____

4. _____   ❑ Continue   ❑ Improve   ❑ New

   _____

5. _____   ❑ Continue   ❑ Improve   ❑ New

   _____

Corporate responsibilities: Most jobs include a range of general responsibilities such as safety, customer service, corporate values, and teamwork. If such issues are important to the organization, they should be discussed in the review.

Goals

1. _____   ❑ Continue   ❑ Improve   ❑ New

   _____

2. _____   ❑ Continue   ❑ Improve   ❑ New

   _____

3. _____   ❑ Continue   ❑ Improve   ❑ New

   _____

4. _____   ❑ Continue   ❑ Improve   ❑ New

   _____

5. _____   ❑ Continue   ❑ Improve   ❑ New

   _____

Index

Selected Titles from the Society for Human Resource Management (SHRM®)

Building Profit through Building People: Making Your Workforce the Strongest Link in the Value-Profit Chain
By Ken Carrig and Patrick M. Wright

Diverse Teams at Work: Capitalizing on the Power of Diversity
By Lee Gardenswartz and Anita Rowe

Essential Guide to Workplace Investigations: How to Handle Employee Complaints & Problems
By Lisa Guerin

Essential Guide to Federal Employment Laws
By Lisa Guerin and Amy Delpo

HR and the New Hispanic Workforce: A Comprehensive Guide to Cultivating and Leveraging Employee Success
By Louis E.V. Nevear and Vaso Perimenis Eckstein

HR Competencies: Mastery at the Intersection of People and Business
By Dave Ulrich, Wayne Brockbank, Dani Johnson, Kurt Sandholtz, and Jon Younger

Igniting Gen B & Gen V: The New Rules of Engagement for Boomers, Veterans, and Other Long-Termers on the Job
By Nancy S. Ahlrichs

Investing in People: Financial Impact of Human Resource Initiatives
By Wayne Cascio and John Boudreau

Solving the Compensation Puzzle: Putting Together a Complete Pay and Performance System
By Sharon K. Koss

Strategic Staffing: A Comprehensive System of Effective Workforce Planning, 2nd ed.
By Tom Bechet

Trainer's Diversity Source Book: 50 Ready-to-Use Activities from Icebreakers through Wrap Ups
By Jonamay Lambert and Selma Myers

TO ORDER SHRM BOOKS

SHRM offers a member discount on all books that it publishes or sells. To order this or any other book published by the Society, contact the SHRMStore®.

ONLINE: www.shrm.org/shrmstore

BY PHONE: 800-444-5006 (option #1); or 770-442-8633 (ext. 362); or TDD 703-548-6999

BY FAX: 770-442-9742

BY MAIL: SHRM Distribution Center
P.O. Box 930132
Atlanta, GA 31193-0132
USA

About the Author

Mike Deblieux is President of Mike Deblieux Human Resources, a management-consulting firm and is a nationally recognized human resources management trainer and consultant. He designs and presents training programs on human-resource related issues such as Documenting Discipline, Writing Performance Reviews, Interviewing, Preventing Sexual Harassment, and Equal Opportunity. Mike provides a full range of HR consulting services to companies of all sizes. He writes and updates employee handbooks and personnel policy manuals.

Mike is an Instructor for the University of California, Irvine Extension Human Resources Management Certificate Program. The Extension has honored him with its Distinguished Instructor Award.

In addition, Mike is a Course Leader for the American Management Association, The Employers Group, the Society for Human Resource Management, and the Professionals in Human Resources Association (PIHRA). In 2002 he was President of PIRHA. He presents nearly 200 programs each year to a variety of private, public, regional, state, and local organizations.

Mike has co-authored the books *Documenting Employee Discipline, Supervisor's Guide to Documenting Discipline*, and *Supervisor's Guide to Performance Reviews*. He is author of the books *Documenting Discipline, Legal Issues for Managers: Essential Skills for Avoiding Your Day in Court*, and *Stopping Sexual Harassment before It Starts*.

Using the Accompanying CD-ROM

For your convenience, all of the performance appraisal forms in the book are on the accompanying CD-ROM. The forms are usable on either a PC or a Macintosh computer. Forms are included in two formats: Portable Document Format and Rich Text Format.

Portable Document Format (PDF) Files

The PDF files contain the forms exactly as they appear in the book—with all formatting. To open the files and print them out, all you need is the free Adobe® Acrobat® Reader, which is included on the CD-ROM. See "Getting Started," below. To customize or modify the PDF forms, you need the full Adobe® Acrobat® system. If you do not have that program on your computer, you can get information and purchase it from www.acrobat.com.

Rich Text Format (RTF) Files

The RTF files contain all of the text of the forms but not all of the formatting. RFT files can be opened in many word processing programs and provide an easy-to-modify version of the forms.

Acrobat Reader 5.0.5 System Requirements

The PDF files on this disc are compatible with Acrobat Reader versions 4.0 and higher.

On the PC

- Intel® Pentium® processor
- Microsoft® Windows® 95 OSR 2.0, Windows 98 SE, Windows Millennium, Windows NT® 4.0 with Service Pack 5, Windows 2000, or Windows XP
- 64 MB of RAM
- 24 MB of available hard-disk space
- Additional 70 MB of hard-disk space for Asian fonts (optional)

On the Macintosh

- PowerPC® processor
- Mac OS software version 8.6*, 9.0.4, 9.1, or OS X*
- 64 MB of RAM
- 24 MB of available hard-disk space
- Additional 70 MB of hard-disk space for Asian fonts (optional)

* Some features may not be available due to OS limitations

Getting Started

To access the files on the CD-ROM, follow the applicable process below.

On the PC

Insert the CD-ROM into your compact disc drive. The disc will AutoRun and prompt you to install Acrobat Reader 5.0.5, if required, or open the Main Menu. Follow the directions on your screen.

On the Macintosh

Insert the CD-ROM into your compact disc drive. Double-click on the *Install Acrobat Reader 5.0.5* icon, select *Custom Install*, check the *Acrobat Reader 5.0* and *Search* boxes, and click the *Install* button. After Acrobat is installed, double-click on the Main-Menu.pdf file to start.

STOP!

Please read the following before opening the CD-ROM accompanying this book.

This software contains files to help you use the sample forms described in the accompanying book. By opening the CD-ROM package, you are agreeing to be bound by the following agreement:

Once you open the seal on the software package, this book and the CD-ROM are nonrefundable. (With the seal unbroken, the book and CD-ROM are refundable only under the terms generally allowed by the seller.)

This software product is protected by copyright and all rights are reserved by the Society for Human Resource Management (SHRM*) and its licensors. You are licensed to use this software on a single computer. Copying the software to another medium or format for use on a single computer is permitted and therefore does not violate the U.S. Copyright Law. Copying the software for any other purposes is not permitted and is therefore a violation of the U.S. Copyright Law.

This software product is sold as is without warranty of any kind, either express or implied, including but not limited to the implied warranty of merchantability and fitness for a particular purpose. Neither SHRM nor its dealers or distributors assumes any liability for any alleged or actual damages arising from the use of or the inability to use this software. (Some states do not allow the exclusion of implied warranties, so the exclusion may not apply to you if you receive this product in such a state.)